THROUGH THE RAIN AND RAINBOW

Through rain and rainbows let us walk
And pause and ponder as we talk
Of beauty, burning like an ember,
That you see . . . and I remember.

Let us lean against the sky
Westward where the echoes die,
Each sound that your quick ear gives
Sifted for me through silent sieves . . .

—*Richard Kinney*

THROUGH THE RAIN AND RAINBOW

The Remarkable Life Of
RICHARD KINNEY

Lyle M. Crist

Lima • *FAIRWAY PRESS* • *Ohio*

THROUGH THE RAIN AND RAINBOW

Library of Congress Cataloging in Publication Data

CRIST, LYLE M.
    Through the rain and rainbow.

    1. Kinney, Richard, 1923-   2. Blind-deaf—
Biography. I. Title.
HV1792.K55C7   362.4'1'0924 [B]   73-22386

ISBN 0-687-42036-9

this book is dedicated to
all the Dick Kinneys
who, in their own manner,
express dominion
over the sense of limitation

PREFACE

This story probably began in 1954 when I became a new faculty member at Mount Union College. It was the year of Dick Kinney's graduation.

Many others have been closer to him through the years, know more of his deepest thoughts, certainly have shared directly in his travail and achievement. None, however, has been more impressed with his wit, his insight, and the lessons to be learned from knowing him.

My portrait of him is colored with my own thought as a teacher (though Dick was not a student of mine) as well as friend. The magnetic awareness of his achievement —initially discerned when I sat among other robed faculty members listening to his eloquence at the senior farewell— was realized more fully when I had a chance to chat with him about one of his poems. It was a simple descriptive stanza about the sunset, surely one of the most common of poetic references, yet so beautifully imaged by this man who cannot see and cannot hear.

He told me, "The problem with most people is that they forget everything they saw and heard yesterday, thinking always about how much more there is to see and hear tomorrow. They pass right by the beauties of today."

You will find the poem later in these pages. The book stems from my desire not to let the beauty—yes, I think that's the perfect word for this man's life—pass by others. I do not want it sentimentalized, for it is not that, but if you sense emotion and admiration, let them be acknowledged now, for surely they are part of my view of this remarkable man.

Lyle Crist

CONTENTS

MORNING

He had flown before, to Rome, to Oslo, and to London, and he would fly across the globe many times in years to come. A figure of international stature, leader of those who most of all need a guide.

For him flying was a particularly invigorating experience, the motion of the airliner holding special treats. The newfound push against the seat in gentle roll as wings shift in angled turn; lift and fall in buoyant moments that come with cloud layers that press themselves against the metal shell; the message of the tire touch on concrete runway. Dick Kinney knew this airport and the vast channels of airways and their motion. He had been aloft before with business associates and in future years he would be an emissary to Japan, to Spain, to India.

He was not alone on this bright early summer morning as the cab approached O'Hare Field, northwest of the Chicago loop. He reached out and held the hand of the woman next to him. The driver catching a glimpse through the mirror, knew he had two special passengers.

How very special? June 16, 1962. The couple had been picked up at the nearby Sheraton Motel where they had stayed the night before. Now, easing into the high upper ramp, the cab stopped. Luggage was put on a rack by a porter; they began walking into the terminal. 9 A.M.

His arm was on hers. They strode into the mass of persons.

On a smooth white terrazzo floor hundreds walked. Eyes were on television screens above, departure times and gate arrivals posted. Below, serpentine channels brought luggage from incoming flights and more hundreds hurried by, grabbed suitcases, and moved to the bright day outside.

United, Braniff, TWA, Delta, Eastern. Rows of counters and lines by each. The public address system droned names. Benches full of old men and women and sailors on leave and toddlers playing tag, unaware of jets and flaps and transponders and radar screens. The porter pushed the luggage cart, and the couple followed. People were looking at ceilings and children with balloons and television screens with gate numbers and escalator steps appearing and disappearing; with these they do not notice this couple, his arm on her arm as they move ahead.

There are so many people, one more couple does not make a difference. Even the bond of travel does not link all. We live in shells, even in airport terminals. We hide ourselves, or we push ourselves. In crowds we withdraw and close our eyes and become alone, even as the elements around us. Fluorescent lights are caged in ceiling panels and newspapers are pushed into bins. And who is to notice two people who stride forward this morning to reach out?

It is inside that he notices. Everything is inside from his arm to his shoes; the jostling is helpful, for here are people, and it is how they touch that makes them people. The slide of fabric across his coat, the encounter with another's shoes, the height of every movement that he feels. Cadence continues like some morning walk, and the sloping floor bends away now, calling for adjustments, a too-heavy thrust on her arm. Jostling is good with adjustments.

Beyond the counters, on the way to the spiderleg concourses now to gates E and F past the newsstand and beauty parlor. "Cosmetics" on one sign and "USO" on the other, but they do not make mention of these; the bending floor means more to both of them.

Luggage checked, porter paid. Holding hands now, they are swallowed again by the crowd which moves in knots headed for London and Geneva and Miami and New York and Milwaukee. A cleaning man with supplies reflects upon them briefly; he will sweep red carpet by the departure gates, clean pillars, dust chairs. He has four more gates to go, and it is after 9:15 now, and he does not give much pause to couples in the concourse.

Black panel walls with blocks of aggregate contrasting. Glistening walls and a poster advertising the glories of Hawaiian surf, another the thrills of Las Vegas. Real estate developers with briefcases hurry by, and a white poodle with a rhinestone collar gets more attention than this couple, now paused at the gate. He is thirty-nine years old, rounded, a relatively short man, a bit hesitant in movement. She is twenty-eight, slightly taller than he, willowy, more confident in stride. Her eyes appear bright, head held high. Planes take off every forty seconds from O'Hare, and the luggage belts disgorge overnighters in endless streams, and people watch for the flight numbers, and they notice the veterans and the cleaning man and the very young couples. But few take notice of these two people.

She hands their tickets to the blue-clad representative and smiles. Her eyes have a distinctive aura; there is anticipation but that is not all. Stamping the tickets, the agent comments on their seat numbers, returns the tickets —and only then senses what that aura may mean.

Confirming times, ready to move into the waiting area until time for boarding, the young woman turns to Dick Kinney, puts her right hand into his palm and moves fingers rapidly, in configurations deliberate and sequential.

Later as sleek wings knife through the bright June skies, the couple holds hands in pauses when her fingers are not moving in those sequential patterns. The couple across the aisle suspect, and the stewardess knows. The seat back begins to press against Dick's back in sustained manner, the metal shell shifts and Dick turns to her and observes, "A climb, all right. I like it!"

Fingers press again, then fingers tracing window outline, touch of fabric again moving slightly across his back. What is it like to be fully aware? What kinds of walls are here, and how are they removed? Those in the terminal have not seen these two people who have seen in each other more than most will be aware of; all seeing is not of the eyes, and there are ways of building walls around us, and there are ways of overcoming walls. Infinities of lonelinesses and infinities of dominions.

Never lonely in their vacuum world, these two people at O'Hare Field, a night together, and a new world opening on this flight.

Mr. and Mrs. Richard Kinney. On their honeymoon to San Francisco.

She is totally blind. He is totally blind.

And he is totally deaf.

And they are very much in love.

VOIDS

He had his sight for seven years. As a teen-ager, having gone through the experience of being told he would lose his eyesight, sensing the curtain falling more each day, until darkness overwhelmed, he knew deprivation.

He knew dominion as well. One afternoon while he still had his hearing his mother said, "There's a crippled bird in the front yard. Looks like it has a broken wing. Hopping around, that's all." Dick thought deeply about the scene, later he found relationship between the bird and himself. Handicap must not deprive him of rightful achievement. He wrote ostensibly of the bird, in actuality of himself:

POOR ROBIN

How did it happen? No one knows.
Hopping across the lawn she goes
With one wing drooping. I suppose
She'll never fly again. The sky
Must seem to her so very high
When other robins hurry by,
Singing, with buoyant wings a-whir,
On homely tasks, bustle and stir,

15

Voids

Joys that will never be for her. . . .
Yet as I muse in pity, she
Goes hopping onward merrily,
To pause at length by the small fir tree.
From ground to lowest bough she springs
And mounts toward heaven without wings—
One branch at a time, she hops and clings.
Now nestlings waken from their naps:
I am confounded—Well, perhaps
She's never heard of handicaps.

To be blind and deaf—to know only by fleeting memory the appearance of the world, the sounds of its teeming expressions, the colors of its moods: how would this affect you and me? To have known in our earliest days the richness of those two key senses, then to be deprived of them just when life begins to realize meaning and purpose might send us into permanent self-pity, introspective isolation.

Achievement might seem so far beyond our reach that we would stop trying to find it.

Dick Kinney has expressed himself in many ways: the lecture platform, teaching, poetry, a comprehensive guide for the deaf-blind. He is a global traveler, representative of the United States government, consultant to governments in South America, Europe, the Orient. Searcher for those living out purposeless lives because of the ignorance of others.

To know of him is to appreciate not only his triumphs against adversity, but also to reach a greater awareness of the possibilities of the triumphs of many other persons as well. You can't help but reach out to others when you get to know this man. He reaches.

And he knows, better than any sighted, hearing person

that it takes a reaching out as well as a remembering to find meaning in life.

"The trouble with most people," he has said, "is that they forget everything they saw and heard yesterday, thinking always about how much more there is to see and hear tomorrow. They pass right by the beauties of today."

He will tell you, "I write of one sunset and one sound of rain and one beautiful rainbow because, unlike you, I never had the chance to forget!"

Perhaps much of what his story conveys is revealed in his poem of a "sunshine-dappled day" which speaks so much of his own dominion. The deep personal meaning of the poem comes in full sweep of his story. Now, however, note these lines:

> *Through rain and rainbows let us walk*
> *And pause and ponder as we talk*
> *Of beauty, burning like an ember,*
> *That you see . . . and I remember.*

What beauty? And what talk?

Unable to see, unable to hear, how does one establish communication? In writing one of the first guides for learning to live with a deaf-blind person, Dick Kinney has pointed to a little child. A toddler, after all, takes our hands, leads us to what he is interested in; he places his toys in our hands, he takes us to the kitchen for water, pats our cheeks when he is happy, hugs us when he wants to show affection. Gestures. Touches.

And that is what the deaf-blind have. It is what we all have but seldom realize, this mystical sense of touch which leads and guides and probes and establishes communication so effectively.

Nineteen years before his honeymoon, Dick Kinney first fully knew the void of deaf-blindness. Losing sight at the age of seven, he concluded schooling in the matchbox town of East Sparta, some sixty miles south of Cleveland, Ohio, and enrolled in Mount Union College nearby, only to realize his fading hearing would not allow him to finish his sophomore year. In 1943 he found himself, after a long, lonely drive back to the family home in the little town, forced to rely on the sense of touch almost exclusively. First the touch of parents, of his sister Rosemary, as they led him; then the fingertip poetry of the Braille dots.

He heard little in 1943. He learned that much of conversation was dependent upon his willingness to lead the discussion. A tap or two from other persons could provide answers directly—if he had asked the right questions. A single tap for "yes," a double tap for "no." The simplest touch giving positive, direct confirmation or reservation.

He had to learn to lead. Touch would lead, but his own mentality would lead even before the touch.

"Nice of you to ask me out for a walk this evening," he might say. "Is it raining out?"

Single tap.

"Oh? Very hard?"

Two taps.

"Good. Well, I'd better have my raincoat anyway. Do I need anything else? Galoshes?"

Double tap.

"Fine. Do you know where the Green Lantern is?"

Single tap.

"Let's take a walk out there. Much traffic on the street tonight?"

Double tap.

"We'll be careful anyway."

He could also wear a white glove with letters marked along the fingers in black ink; friends could touch the letters, slowly spell out words. He had been alerted to this approach to communication during the past year, memorized positions and alphabetical sequence, starting with the thumb tip, down the thumb, then the forefinger tip, down the forefinger, and the others as well. Twenty-six placements in sequence.

There are 16,000,000 blind persons in the world today. The common bleak, sameness of a dark world is overcome in diverse ways; but the blind usually have another common element—most of them have lost their sight after reaching maturity, after having years and segments of years of seeing. Those who lose their hearing as well as sight, some 300,000 in the world, also usually have had their hearing in earlier years—probably 80 percent or more of the deaf-blind have gone through a time sequence comparable to that which befell Dick Kinney.

Even while it happened to him, however, one person who had never reached maturity with sight and hearing was taking steps which would directly affect him. Helen Keller in 1945 was urging the American Foundation for the Blind to establish some kind of system of services for the deaf-blind. Having served as a consultant to the AFB since 1923, she was asking for greater involvement and was being heard. In 1945 she met with an advisory committee to outline the scope of the work, asking for greater research for communication mechanisms, more funds for educational purposes, more career counseling and practical assistance so that the deaf-blind could become more self-sufficient. Had all approaches to hearing aids been explored? Were Braille watches, Braillewriters sufficiently available, made known, as efficient as possible? The AFB, established as an independent national organization in

1921, was, she felt, the logical agency to step out to dramatically aid the deaf-blind. The years were formative; the deaf-blind registry for 1945 showed an increasing awareness on the part of referring agencies in most of the states.

And Dick Kinney, sometimes able to hear brief portions of the "School of the Air" on radio, thought about his classmates at Mount Union who would receive their diplomas as he sat in isolation.

You sit. There is nothing around you except the touch of the chair, the feel of the sidewalk, the nudge of your sister, the taste of homemade pie. There is no sight, no sound in a teeming world—even in East Sparta where stickball is a memory, the roar of motorcycles now a void.

Your mother is home all the time now, helping. If she goes to the yard to hang out clothing she tells you, either shouting in your ear or tapping out letters to spell words on the white gloves. Sometimes she will go to another part of the house briefly, when you start a conversation, a commentary of yours for her. You talk and receive no reply, but you are sharing a thought with her and then the wooden floor under your chair vibrates and then again.

Mother is in the basement. She has heard your voice but wants you to know she can't have conversation of any kind right now. She is rapping the floor with a broom from the basement.

Oh, well, you didn't know. You were talking to four blank walls.

And one floor that thumps an awkward message.

Is that all there is to be? Will you sit there the rest of your life, depending on tastes and nudges and touches?

Will you forget all that you had learned at Mount Union College in a brief year and a half?

Forget all about writing, about poetry that had been

so much a part of English classes? Could you never share symbol and word?

The world of Dick Kinney's mind became sharper as he waited out lonely days and years, groping for purpose. He turned to poetry, as he had before, to find expression for his thoughts. Creatively oriented persons move to that mental arena where one frame of reference is used to express another—saying one thing in terms of another, the coupling of ideas, comparisons. Such becomes basic in poetry writing. To see pictures is not sufficient for the poet; it is always the using of those pictures in context with something else that enables pyramiding of knowledge, widening understanding.

But first the images. In high school, as his sight was gone and hearing fading into inevitable oblivion, Dick had found the night time of stark, blatant colors. He had used them metaphorically as birds. He had written:

THEN NIGHT CAME DOWN

Then night came down on raven wings
and slew the white dove, day;
in talons taut with vulture winds
*   he wrested her away.*
The western hills ran red with blood,
as to celestial wars:
The eastern sky was dusked behind
With white pinfeather stars . . .

A "picture poem," with strong indications of depression in it. The raven slays, winds are vultures, and celestial wars abound.

During this long, searching time for Dick he wrote many times of the night, of somber skies, of celestial activities. The following poem from this same era is of beauty,

21

but its indirectness of imagery again suggests it is of more than beauty:

DIM BEAUTY

The pallid splendor of the moon
   Whispers to the sky
The silver drift of stardust strewn
On the hollow heave of the long lagoon
   Slumbers in the eye.
Yet the pensive moon is fair
For all the pallor of her hair
And the sifting star-clouds rise
Like incense smoke from Paradise.

Beauty need not burn to shimmer,
   Nor the heart to pine
I sometimes think of two the dimmer
Is the fairer far; the glimmer
   of a glowworm's shrine,
As by some unseen angel spun
Outlasts the glory of the sun,
For ever the cult of the sun-ray find
A burning glance, and love turned blind.

No one can blame the writer for sensing the night time in his own experience. The sun indeed, unseen, burned as love turned blind for him.

He was a young man in torment, catching sounds some days, nothing the next. Like some awesome yo-yo, his hearing would come and go, taunting him, tantalizing him. Holding his ear tightly to the radio he could pick up—on some days, some hours—the sound of the baseball games. He loved the game, drew upon his recollections from childhood, kindled the fascination of throwing the ball with the great players.

On Sunday afternoons, when sounds came in no measure, he sat in the back yard under the elm trees and asked his father to keep him informed about the Cleveland Indians. He loved the players' names: Lou Boudreau, Ken Keltner, Bob Feller were among his favorites. Hobart Kinney, from whom the lure of baseball had been acquired, found pleasure in touching his son's fingers in the glove. This was something they could "talk" about readily, sharp abbreviated words of the father speeding up communication, Dick seeing in his mind's eye the action at Cleveland stadium.

Someday, maybe tomorrow, he would hear again.

He held to that possibility. Even as, a decade before, he had held to the chance of additional sight.

It was time, however, to learn of a better way of silent dialogue. Myrtle Wells, home teacher for the blind, working for the state of Ohio, came to the Kinney house for that purpose. Blind since birth, she had a driver take her from home to home on a visitation schedule. She was a valuable, active person in her assignment. Told of a young man in East Sparta who, now blind, was losing hearing as well, she visited the Kinney home. Yes, Hope Kinney said, her son did hear a sound once in a while, did try the Sonotone on occasion, but now, in 1947—years had moved on in quiet ways—he had only spasmodic results. His isolation was almost entire.

Even the slightest return of sounds added problems; Dick was less than enthusiastic about learning the manual touch communication system—the briefest of sounds still gave him slight hope. Learning the manual was psychologically bad, he felt, signaling a finality. Miss Wells brought in her own psychological approach, suggesting that the manual be learned as a new skill to sharpen his mind.

Fingers placed in the palm; the first for "A," the thumb crooked for "B," tips in loose arc for "C," then a clenching of three fingers, outstretching of the forefinger and a straight thumb for "D" . . . now doing these again, now in sequence, then on to the next in the alphabet, then the simplest of words—as in kindergarten—"B-A-D" and "D-A-D" and now start again.

He worked with the configurations, practiced them with his mother, then worked again when Miss Wells returned another week. Hope Kinney was, of course, invaluable, patient, leading him. In a month or so the manual was mastered. It had the extra personal ingredient; other helps, an early version of the Braille transcriber, for instance, were too mechanical. The manual, very personal, had been dramatized through the widely publicized story of Helen Keller. If there were no shred of hope for hearing, there was new hope in this communication.

His mother and sister mastered the manual; his father, Hobart, finding his fingers too cumbersome from years of being a catcher in semipro baseball, preferred the white glove.

Historically, the manual had developed slowly, with a variety of adaptations since medieval times. According to most sources, it began as a series of simple touches among the monks who had taken solemn vows of silence during their monastic periods. It became more sophisticated, evolving into a letter-reference rather than a word-reference series of touches, allowing for greater complexity of thought.

Dick was encouraged at this time by Miss Wells to speak out whenever the slightest reception of sound seemed possible; to hear his own voice so that modulation could become a mental judgment rather than one of sound.

Soon there would be no more sound for him. The last sputtering sounds, jagged and tedious to catch, were in 1948. For highest dramatic purposes, they should have been of some loving statement within the family, or the laughter of a friend, the sound of nature—a bird, dog, leaves in the wind. For him it was not this dramatic, however, though, in perspective, perhaps appropriate. The Cleveland Indians won the World Series in October of 1948. Hearing aid glued to the radio, he heard scattered sounds of announcers during the last game.

He has never heard a sound since then.

Five years had elapsed since the lonely twenty-five-mile trip back to East Sparta from Mount Union College. Years to reminisce about the school, think of classes and campus, times to ponder whether he could ever pick up the pieces. Secretly, he nourished the thought of classes again. Manual gained, he needed only other persons to know it as well. Everything was of his mind now, within himself, but the reaching out of the manual was necessary—and he longed to reach out again. He thought many times of the campus and its diverse ways of learning. He pondered the college.

He had known the campus of Mount Union College, some fifty-four acres in the friendly industrial town of Alliance, dotted with three nineteenth-century vestiges of Orville Nelson Hartshorn's initial school founded in 1854. Proud of Methodist heritage, the school offered a liberal arts curriculum to its 850 students. The buildings were all of red brick, aged in appearance—a right mix of architecture and time to produce the atmosphere of academic enterprise, almost hoary. To the front of the campus two lakes complemented the colonial facade of the women's dormitory.

From the beginning he had a career in mind that would be based on English. Perhaps a combination of writing and teaching. A degree was essential, part of a liberating (even more than "liberal") process, at once freeing from the limitation of blindness yet molding and shaping his future. He had given college a good try in 1941 when he enrolled in the fall as a freshman. For a year and a half he had no void.

Back then, with hearing aid firmly attached, he relied on Tom Maxwell for reading certain of his lessons. As he had in high school, his texts were Brailled in special editions. Maxwell had started his own college career at Mount Union during the summer session that year, found an offer through the admissions office to help a young blind student not only a good one for the companionship and assistance he could give, but also for income; in exchange for rooming with Dick Kinney he would receive his board. To read the lessons to Dick, the state of Ohio would pay enough to go a long way towards his tuition.

They met in the fall, shared the room, main floor at Miller Hall, first on the left down the relatively short, narrow hallway. Maxwell knew of some teasing that his young charge had to put up with. One fellow in particular delighted in deluding him by calling to Dick and then moving, or by punching him and then stepping back. It was the cruelest of jokes, but it took time to bring understanding to that student. Maxwell made it his task to do so.

In other directions, Dick found time to keep his thought on Gloria Haverman, who had been a favorite friend during his high school days. She received many letters from him during that freshman year, nearly all of them lighthearted. Maxwell would leave for service that year—and so would most of the other young men whom he got to know during the year. Mount's campus, like other small campuses, was being drained of men. He summarized the dilemma with regard to one of his courses in a letter to Gloria:

Twelve hours of science is required here; I suggested that physics would be a nice study. "Well, you know, Mr. Kinney," protested the Dean, "college physics is a very complicated course, laboratory work, fancy diagrams, and things like that. I suggest you take the simplified course we give here called 'Man and the Nature of His Physical World.' It's along the same lines as physics, only less technical."

"Man and the Nature of His Physical World!" Why, *man* hasn't a thing to do with it! The first morning last week when I took my place in class Dr. Shollenberger, the professor in charge, walked calmly in, glanced about the room, and began his lecture: "Ladies, and Mr. Kinney . . ."

Later Dick suggested that if Gloria were ever to enroll, she might well be advised to take the easy course in "Woman and the Nature of Her Physical World."

He could laugh at himself, and even write as though he had full vision. To Gloria he described a speech contest held one afternoon, competition for seven-minute orations which he entered. He wrote as follows:

Casually we strolled into the lecture room, widening the doorway on the way in. I mean I widened the doorway. Taking my stance in front of the room, I surveyed the scene before me with the practiced eye of a man used to dealing with emergencies. At the far end of the room, behind an imposing table, sat three somber-faced judges, eyeing me in the same way that Kelly would a canary. After a moment's impressive pause, and in a voice both soft and suave, my poise superb and manner polished, I began my stirring address. As the rich, clear tones of that well-modulated voice slowly filled the room, I could sense my audience leaning forward, their faces rapt with attention. I was in rare form. Slowly, with an unhurried flow, the golden stream of my address for six poignant minutes poured forth. Then, beholding the six-minute sign, I dashed out a brilliant metaphor, soared a dizzy flight on oratorical rhetoric, and casting one more dazzling smile in the direction of the judges, I took my graceful departure.

The daily walks across the campus green, the unseen Gothic style of Chapman Hall, the muffled creaking of its slatted floors, the narrow, winding stairways, worn stone steps, the ancient panelling along corridor walls—these mixed in his thought with the recollections of early years in East Sparta, clear, vivid scenes which remained in the years of blindness. He mused as well on the patch of yellow buttercups he remembered in the field by his home.

And a rainbow over outbuildings across the railroad track.

"I have read novels in which the hero is blind, and you keep hearing the muffled sobs and cries of the parents in the background. Not so with me, not so with so many others; the crying remains inside. We came to accept it and to work with it, not against the blindness."

Miller Hall became a dormitory for air force cadets who were coming to campus for preflight training. In turn, Dick moved out of Miller Hall and into the Sigma Nu fraternity house on the rim of the campus. Charles "Jiggs" Evans became his guide, a tall, southern-accented pre-med student.

Dick wrote to a friend that he had been examined for service and that the Army, Navy, and Marine Corps all wanted him to join! "The Army wanted me to join the Navy, and the Navy wanted me to join the Marines, and the Marines wanted me to join the Army!"

To Gloria he wrote more delightful letters of wit and description. In late winter he told her,

Last Friday morning I arose bright and early, consumed a hearty breakfast of peanut butter and crackers, combed my curly locks into a graceful wave, and tripped lightly down the stairs on my way to philosophy class. I walked into a blizzard. Snow was piling down from every direction . . . it is three blocks from here to Lamborn Hall. One block and I looked like a bed sheet; two and I looked like a bed sheet's ghost; three and I faintly resembled a snowdrift taking a hike.

Concluding the experience he said, "The storm was nothing to what happened afterward. As you know, I never bother with a hat and this time something tells me it was a mistake. Who would think that my flowing tresses and a common sponge would have so much in common? My hair let go with enough water to irrigate the Sahara Desert or historical geology—both of which are equally dry." His descriptions from that freshman year abound in *pictures*:

This morning this campus witnessed one of the strangest spectacles ever beheld by the eye of man. No, it wasn't three men on a horse; just two men and a typewriter on a bicycle. You see, this morning Jiggs showed up with a bicycle, that is, most of a bicycle. The light was broken, the horn dead, the handlebar rubbers gone, and the brake out of order, but outside of that he said it was in good condition. When I protested that I had to take my typewriter to geology class for a test, he airily waved his hand and assured me with a disdainful smile that we would make it in three minutes. We climbed on, including Beulah, who is, you know, my typewriter. We started out beautifully, down hill. And then, turning the corner, we headed up College Street, a distinctly uphill grade. Every time we hit a bump I left the bicycle in a vertical direction and Beulah left me in the same way. This was bad enough, but then things began to get out of control and the whole swivel-hipped bicycle began to wobble. We not only covered ground, we covered the whole street. I'll swear that our course was so crooked we were in danger of having a

29

wreck from meeting ourselves coming back! What we did would have made a corkscrew dizzy. I'll admit that the pedestrians that we passed were very nice, shouting all kinds of encouragement, or I think it was encouragement. Jiggs yelled for me to hang on, which was a quite unnecessary comment, and then we hit a soft spot in the dirt road. I shall always believe that the U.S. Army missed one of the greatest exhibitions of the technique of modern warfare in human history when they missed what followed. In less than thirty seconds Jiggs and I had dug a trench big enough for half a regiment of infantry to occupy.

He recovered, however, from this and other escapades; he joined the Sigma Alpha Epsilon fraternity and found a place in the social whirl—such as it was—on campus. He dated—and wrote of a young girl falling in love:

FIRST LOVE

Her hopes are like three silent drums
Convulsed with thunder when he comes.
Her fears are like four candle wicks
Consumed by lightning when he speaks.
Her love is like a crimson scroll
Of choral music priests unroll
And little girls in white robes sing.
Her heart is like a swallow's wing.

When the fall of 1943 rolled around he was still game for continuing college, despite further admonitions from physicians that his hearing aid might not provide enough amplification. A "noticeable dip" in his hearing had, indeed, occurred. In summer he brooded at home, experimented with the Sonotone, stayed close to the radio, listening to Fulton Lewis report the war, following episodes of Jack Armstrong, flying fingers over Braille copy of news commentaries as well. And publishing poetry in area newspapers.

He wanted to return to Mount Union—for however long he "could last." There was always the possibility that a "noticeable rise" in hearing might occur. That summer had not, however, given cause for such hopes. He sensed further erosion of hearing on a bountiful summer evening at Atwood Lake, not far from home. Sonotone on, he tried fishing. His dad gave instructions, a booming voice calling out best waters, slightest movements. A familiar voice, readily understood in implication and yet this evening farther away than ever before, remote—at times the merest echo. In retrospect, Dick says, "I'm sure the fish were all duly warned!" The voice, louder, louder, and yet never clearer, never loud enough.

Neither Hope nor Hobart Kinney thought he should return to campus. Matters were too bewildering as incidents of this type recurred through the summer. But he felt strongly about continuing; he wanted all the education he could get.

So he returned. The Sigma Nu house, where he had stayed in the spring, was not available; more air cadets had arrived, gobbling up housing, now even fraternity houses. However, civilians had the Alpha Tau Omega house which was, fortunately, closer to Chapman Hall where most of his classes were scheduled. It was a sturdy, red brick, two-story home overlooking the campus lakes, side door spilling out young men towards Chapman. In the fall of 1943 it was not for fraternity members, but for "the men," the few civilians. One was Bob "Hiney" Hines, now Dick's roommate.

He began a new round of studies, continued correspondence with Gloria, and approached the examination period in January with more A's likely. But his hearing bothered more and more, lectures harder to hear; he knew he was missing more than he was getting. He would tap the Sonotone, talk to it, adjust it, wondering how long he could hold out. Yet he could laugh at himself. To Gloria he described an eventful series of activities on Sunday, December 5, 1943:

Some time during the course of this letter I am likely to collapse into a drunken stupor. No, I haven't touched a drop of Uncle Charley's snakebite medicine, but, well, it's a long story.

The whole thing started because of the unhappy circumstance that the Sunday supper which the college serves isn't quite up to standard. It's the meal when the dietician opens the icebox and sort of sweeps up everything that didn't get eaten during the week—sort of a food salvage drive. Consequently, five or six boys drifted into my room about five o'clock and invited me to go down to Isaly's for supper. Now ordinarily I would have been very happy to accept, but last evening we had a big semi-formal, inter-fraternity dance, and what with taxi fares and tickets and so forth, my financial investments had diminished the personal exchequer. In fact, I had just one paper dollar and a little change to my name.

"Napoleon," I pointed out, "would have given anything to have the food the college will serve tonight when he was starving in Russia."

"Yes," said Dan Wertman, "but it was fresh then." So we went to Isaly's.

Somewhere in my pedigree there must have been a Scotsman —of that I am certain. Furthermore, he must have been a thrifty Scotsman—the kind of man who would pull the chair out from under Whistler's mother to look for small change behind the cushion. I know this has to be because the moment I entered the door, I felt an irresistible instinct to save that dollar bill.

We went to a table and the others ordered malted milks

and sandwiches. I ordered a milkshake and a sandwich. (You can save a nickel by leaving out the malt, which really doesn't add much flavor anyway). "Ah," I thought, "I have made it."

Fate, however, was not yet done, for the others decided to get dessert. I opined that I wasn't hungry. "What!" said Hiney Hines, "you were the guy who was telling me an hour ago you were almost starved." As they continued to press me, I thought feverishly for something that only cost a nickel, for a lone buffalo was all that stood between me and that dollar bill. "EUREKA!" I thought. "I have it!"

The waitress, a cute little blonde, though of course I prefer brunettes myself, came tripping up and asked if we wanted anything else. "Pie," "Pie," "Pie," "Pie," "Buttermilk," came the order. She looked at me in that funny way that people do, and moved away. Soon we had our stuff.

Now really, it's amazing how much buttermilk you get for a nickel! It must have been at least a pint. The boys attacked their pie, and with a confident smile I took a great big swig of buttermilk. Now big sugary glasses of chocolate milkshake and even bigger vinegary mugs of buttermilk have their places, which are certainly not in succession. I realized this instantly. The flavor was sort of, sort of—well—susceptible to improvement. Thinking to improve the situation, I picked up a salt shaker and dumped about half a shakerful in. It was a bad thought. But with my eyes set on the beautiful ideal of saving that fresh, beautiful bill, I started to drink. Strange how full I began to get. The blood slowly rose to my head, my eyes began to pop, and by the time I had finished the last drop, I was ready to. Complaining of a sprained ankle, I leaned on Hiney the whole way home, and now I am sitting at the keyboard of dear little Beulah awaiting my fate. In my shirt pocket, right next to my heart, is the bright little greenback which only the inspired courage of a long line of economical heroes could have saved.

During the Christmas break when he was back home a severe cold settled in his left ear—his "good" ear. But such things occurred before; he held out for some improvement in a week or so. However, no good results came from a variety of tests and treatments. He missed January on campus, but went back for the semester examinations, Hope Kinney Brailling the tests for him on the campus. Dick typed out answers.

His academic work had come to an end.

That last day on campus in early 1944 he could not hear a trace of his own voice, even as he shouted.

The drive back to East Sparta was not a complicated one; from the southern edge of Alliance where the campus was, the drive not more than thirty-five minutes, but for Hope Kinney it was longer that January afternoon than it had ever been before.

In silence they had packed his belongings, started back to the little town, the highway a line guiding Dick into the legions of the deaf-blind, becoming one of perhaps 1,500 in the United States. Or was it twice that figure? No one could tell for sure; the American Foundation for the Blind carried an official register of 1,456 deaf-blind at that time, but because some families hesitate to label publicly their deaf-blind, identification of many is nearly impossible.

Someday Dick Kinney would be one of the leaders in the outreach to identify and help.

But, arriving at East Sparta, he could look forward then only to the touch of family, the night of blindness, the suspended nothingness of deafness.

Time would work on his side. They kept affirming that; his hearing would improve, the war would sometime end, the whole world would improve. They could try new doctors, new treatments; some new drug called penicillin might be of help. Nobody knew just quite what, but the dual loss of sight and hearing had been caused by *some-*

thing, and surely there was *something* which would correct it. The law of averages: if they tried everything, something would be right.

Dick would not merely resign himself to inaction. They would keep on experimenting. The sound of a car, a hit against the bedroom wall, the song of a bird some morning. These would awaken the dormant senses, and things would be all right.

But there was also the quiet recognition of history.

No deaf-blind since Helen Keller had ever been able to earn a college diploma. No one in East Sparta, Alliance, anywhere in the realm of Dick's life was ready to suggest he could ever continue. Air cadets would continue at Mount Union and go off to war flying their planes and having girls sing about the wild blue yonder, capture the headlines and the emotion of the world torn apart by war.

His world had been torn apart in a different, fragile manner.

Could he find purpose in his life?

Someone suggested that a blind person could become a salesman in the home; in high school this was one of the fine "career opportunities" available to him, according to the counselors. He tried this from the home—handling magazine subscriptions. For the first time he utilized his twin handicaps in an appeal for support; it was not like him to do this, but prompted by others he made reference early in one of his solicitation letters sent out from "Richard Kinney's Magazine Service—Lowest Rates, Unexcelled Service":

Suppose you could no longer see or hear. What would you do to earn your living?

My own answer to this problem can mean money saved for you.

In the home, in the office, everyone reads magazines. Many people find it a wise economy to place their subscriptions and renewals through a single reliable agent. Would you care to make me your subscription secretary?

An appropriate magazine subscription can be the perfect gift for almost any occasion, no shopping, no wrapping, no bother! Presents that last all year. Just glance at the enclosed bargain folder.

Through Braille, the typewriter, and the manual alphabet, I can do much of this work myself. What help I need is given by my mother, an efficient partner in assuring you satisfaction.

His business did succeed; it was the first branch of the tree on which the robin was clinging.

Five years went by in slow, tentative findings. His haunted mind began by that time, however, to find solace, even as the finality of deaf-blindness was fully discerned. His resolution is seen in a poem which he wrote near the end of that difficult period. In it he expressed the confidence of a person emerging, buttressing himself now for encounters which he knew he must face without isolation:

WHEN I BEHOLD

When I behold the fearsomeness of night
Emblazoned by a thousand starry gems
And see the awful chasm crowned with light,
A suppliant to heaven's diadems;
When I behold the canopy of good
That overlies the evil dearth below
As if compassionate heaven kindly would
That even the darkest depths some light might know;
I marvel at the portraiture of life,
That one day burns in rapture, then in pain;
That tears itself in sad, periodic strife,
Then struggles up to kiss the peaks again.

Voids

Perceive I thus the glory of these scars;
That life, earthbound, forever seeks the stars.

The poem revealed his hope; one day his life had been rapture, then, indeed, came "sad, periodic strife"; now his earthbound, sense-bound experience was seeking the stars.

He was readying himself to grope for his own stars, somehow to return to formal education. He believed in destiny. "Each time I am buffeted or deflected out of a sense of hidden strengths and purpose, buffeted by circumstances of adversity, I come back to this theme. A compass needle can be deflected, but something within it turns it north again."

Twenty-five years after he wrote "When I Behold" he said, "I always knew that someday I would marry. I really always knew that. Sometimes I had to keep assuring myself, but I believe I always knew that someday I would experience the full measure of love."

Stars have always been symbols of high goals; some people stop looking at them, but not Dick Kinney. He once wrote, "Only the living things that solved their problems successfully enough to have posterity belong in our family tree. We carry within us all the experience, endurance, aspiration, and know-how refined and assimilated by the great, integral lifeline over three billion years, from the first amoeba to ourselves!"

He remembered correspondence he had during high school days with a school for the blind somewhere near Chicago. It had been a question of history then, something further he wanted to read about the Virginia legislature. Getting some material from them, he found out they offered a variety of courses by correspondence for the blind. Now, he wondered, "Could I find out more about poetry from this school?"

Hadley School for the Blind. Well, it might be worth trying. With his typewriter, he began a letter of background, including as well a few of his poems. Perhaps the Hadley School might be able to give him useful instruction and criticism.

Then he waited. A muted waiting. Nature had become isolated vestiges in his memory, jogged in one way by the names of streets in town. East Sparta's streets carried names of trees; perhaps in the wilderness long ago trees abounded. In his silent world with sister or mother guiding he could walk the streets near home—from the Kinney house on Chestnut you would cross Pine, follow it to Main, then turn two blocks to Locust, and then the high school loomed. What part would school ever play now in his world?

His poems, on their way to the Hadley School, were his stars above.

FINDINGS

The packet of poems arrived routinely in the morning mail that autumn day in 1948, at the desk of Donald Wing Hathaway, instructor, graduate of Northwestern University, published poet, head of the English Department of the Hadley School for the Blind. He opened letters with enthusiasm for his work, enjoying the banter by mail with his students. He had been a member of the staff in Winnetka since 1927, seen many students achieve writing skills, some go on to be published, recognized. His own special interests were in English literature, particularly the poetry of the romanticists.

His office was not much more than a closet tucked in a row of rooms that constituted the school, which, surviving on contributions, was long on enthusiasm if not on capital. But he did not need a large classroom for his teaching; the office gave him a Braille typewriter; he needed not much except his own keen insight of student abilities along with that typewriter. He opened the envelope from East Sparta, Ohio, inquiring about a course in verse writing, wondering if the instructor would look over the enclosed poems and see whether he qualified for a class if one were offered.

A poet, eh? Well, we'll see; many write for advice because writing is an activity the blind can handle well. Take a look at the material and see. Hathaway, sighted, could read Braille but was pleased that the copy enclosed was in ink print. The reading would be less complicated.

He lifted out the first of several poems, found it titled "David Sling," and began to read; as he read each line his interest increased, became at the end an excited response:

> *My David sling was but a hope*
> *To counteract a woe,*
> *And three small pebbles shrank in scope*
> *Against Goliath's brow.*
>
> *The first stone fell, a random wish:*
> *The next was but a prayer:*
> *The third sped forth, a bolt of love,*
> *And left me monarch there.*

This was not the work of some idle mind, some mere dabbler in poetry! He read on, read two others in the packet, and found himself exclaiming, perhaps with an undue burst of enthusiasm, "I believe Keats has returned this day!" He left his office, asked several others to join him in the lounge where he read all three poems aloud. The others, too, were impressed. Someone very special had made contact with the Hadley School.

Hathaway replied that same day, encouraging Dick to continue submitting his poems. Their correspondence quickly became more than a normal school-student communication: it was, from the first, a correspondence of two kindred souls.

Among the others impressed by the writings was Dorrance Nygaard, Director of the Hadley School. Soon afterwards he read one of the poems before a convention of the American Association of Workers for the Blind; in the audience that day was another teacher, equally pleased with the quality of the poem. Afterwards, she asked Nygaard for Dick's address and began a correspondence which suggested several Braille magazines to which Dick should submit poems. Though none realized it then, this simple additional outreach was to set in line one more piece of the widening solution to the bleak existence that night time, the raven, the vulture had once symbolized for the poet.

The "bolt of love" would make Dick monarch.

Even as he had said.

But, was he "another Keats"? Was this really a useful comparison?

Years later, Karen Gearreald, blind, Hadley teacher and curriculum director, with a Ph.D. from Harvard with a special interest in the British poets, spoke about Keats. "He was a sensory poet."

Then how could any comparison be made—with one who had been deprived of two key senses?

Karen smiled. She was not disputing the comparison. She knew much more than her questioner did at that moment.

Hathaway's interest in Dick prompted much correspondence. Lessons were highly personal commentaries which covered the range of poetry; they prompted witty responses from the student who found both a receptive criticism for his talents and a vital new outlet for his intellectual energies.

For the instructor their bond, stronger with each lesson, made him want to talk directly with Dick. A visit with him would be just great. There were further ways he might be of help, of course, through closer contact; Hadley teachers frequently made educational trips in the cause of the blind. More to the point, however, Hathaway was so intrigued by his student's wit and talent he was drawn to explore the personality even more.

1949. A trip to Ohio was planned that summer. Hathaway on Greyhound to a place called East Sparta. He would go to the little town to learn more of his prize student. He wanted to know more of the story that had begun there some twenty-six years before.

In 1923 East Sparta was large enough to support one school, three churches, and a small cluster of stores. Born there was Hobart Kinney, baseball enthusiast, big-boned, reliable catcher for several semipro teams. He was a class-mate of Hope Rice; their marriage in 1922 came when Hobart was a salesman for a Canton hardware firm. On June 21, 1923 their first child was born—normal, healthy, "a bit plump," and radiating the warmth of the home his parents provided. They named him Donald Richard Kinney.

Four years later initial evidence brought concern for his hardiness. First there were clues that sight was lessening in the right eye. And there were nagging bouts with inflammation in his knees, with frequent fevers.

In 1929, with only one eye functioning, Dick entered the school at East Sparta, his father by this time established in his own hardware business in the village, the family in a white frame home on Chestnut Street, and a new sister, Rosemary, now age two, complementing the family.

"Eye inflammation" continued, and by February of 1930 the boy found it almost impossible to concentrate on the written words or even the picture pages in his books. School officials were puzzled; they had not encountered such a boy as this, such a problem. Doctors were puzzled; perhaps this was some atypical form of arthritis.

Mrs. Kinney had taught the early grades before her own children came: it was natural that she tutor the child through that first year; and thus between her and the teacher Dick was able to conclude his first-year activities, although his sight was minimal at the conclusion of that year.

Then, led by physicians to keep her son out of school, Hope Kinney became more than the "helping teacher"; she became his only teacher for the next four years while solutions to his near blindness were sought.

When you're going blind at the age of six, you look for special ways to prevent the void. For Dick it was a game of ball against the side of the house; he could follow the path of the oversized ball dimly. And once he got to the sidewalk he could sense the necessary path to follow to keep on that walk.

He got the jump on others at his age as far as schooling preparation was concerned. Parents read much to him, more than his friends received. In later life, he said, "They say the way to train a colt to be a winner as a racehorse is to let him win races when he's young." In early grades, through high school, others looked to him for answers, answers which came out of a deep and thorough reading that went back to those earliest days when Hope Kinney would settle back in a living room chair and read and read stories and poems and articles to the child who was learning to run races in his own very special way.

It was his good fortune to be born into the right family; they knew how to treat him. It was hard, yet in retrospect Dick is definite in saying that a sense of hardiness is necessary if the blind person is to make his own way later on. "It works in several ways," he says. "For instance, I can never recall hearing my parents express dismay over my handicap. You'd think that maybe once I would hear Mother sobbing or Dad expressing great sorrow. But they kept that to themselves. For me, they never mentioned their tensions about it."

Dick learned not to lean on favoritism for his own achievements. He learned that within his own consciousness he had all he would ever need, despite the physical handicaps.

Attempts to rehabilitate the child physically continued. Canton Hospital, Akron Children's Hospital, the Cleveland Clinic followed within the year. Then a long trip to Johns Hopkins Wilmer Institute in Baltimore. There was deterioration of nerves in the eyes, ears. No specific name. Someone said rheumatic arthritis. Another told of a similar case in which the boy, stronger physically, overcame it. Brucellosis was also mentioned. Dick still had some vision—awareness of some colors, some differences between walks and grass, but he was unable to read.

Yet after first grade he was surprised he wasn't allowed to go back to school. "I still had one good eye." But then slow blindness like a fog came occasionally over that eye. "I remember telling Mother I couldn't see and hadn't been able to see for several days. She said it might be better tomorrow, but like a mist, it didn't really ever lift after that. I could still see some light, guess I even rode my tricycle a bit."

A new school authority came to town. Dick was ten years old when W. J. Snitzer took over as superintendent of the East Sparta schools, heard about the young Kinney boy who was unable to come to school with his classmates, the first blind boy the village had ever known. Too bad about having to stay home like that. Snitzer was surprised at the lack of steps taken by the school system to assist;

he knew of other cases and set about to see what he could do. First he contacted the Ohio Commission for the Blind, inquiring of ways formal education might be continued and the financing of them. Yes, there was a special school in Cleveland where a young boy could attend and learn the Braille system of communication; he'd need that, of course, to keep pace with any textbook reading. Braille copies could be arranged for him—there were volunteer agencies to assist their preparation, if titles were not already in Braille. But such services were of no use if the boy did not know Braille. The Waring School it was called, in Cleveland. Sixty miles north. The boy could take a bus, go there for special training and then return to follow his classes in Braille.

To learn Braille.

He began in September, 1934, finding himself at age eleven boarding at a private home, taking a streetcar to the Waring School, learning the special techniques they offered in helping the visually impaired. They would give him grade school instruction and—most important—they would teach him Braille and the relationship of Braille to his subjects.

It was not a completely happy year for the youngster. The arrangement at Waring provided many frustrations. To be near his family, Dick would be placed on a bus each Friday afternoon for the two and a half hour ride back to East Sparta. Then, after a weekend of being with his parents, resuming contact with his home and his family, he would again be placed on the bus every Sunday afternoon for the trip back to Cleveland. And he rode alone each time.

"Quite traumatic, really," Dick recalls. "As a child I was going and coming; just as I'd begin to get used to being away five days I'd be home again, and then have to leave on Sunday afternoon once again." Home was great, school was useful, but the continual displacement played havoc with him.

And yet another perspective would have to form. In January, 1935—midway in his year at Waring—there was a day when he noticed something else slipping away. In class he had handled the Braille dots satisfactorily, learned the touch for reading, but he had to strain to hear the teacher, one day finding his effort more than previous inquiry. He was not hearing satisfactorily. "A noticeable dip," as he phrased it, set the stage for possible further trauma. Not the end of all things, for Dick was still leaping forward in things academic, making up for lost time, perhaps not fully comprehending what the "dip" forecast.

But he finished the year at Waring, ready to return in the next fall to the sixth grade in the little East Sparta school—he had leaped from second to fifth at Waring in a matter of months. Rosemary, now in the second grade, would walk with him from the house on Chestnut Street to school, then guide him home for lunch. The distance was not great—no distance in East Sparta was. Hope Kinney would meet him at the school at the close of classes so that Rosemary might have opportunity for play with her own classmates for part of the day.

Dick and Rosemary concocted games on their walks to school. "We took great pride," she says, "in the fact that we would negotiate steps, curbs, and corners without holding hands. It was just arm against arm—barely touching."

Conversation, too, just "touched" in its own way. Ernie Murray, one of Dick's closest pals in high school years, visited the Kinney house regularly, got involved in checkers and chess with Dick (using a three-dimensional board Hobart had constructed). Ernie frequently walked to school with Dick; their personalities blended, and Ernie, with a sympathetic awareness, knew when Dick's hearing bothered him, both physically and psychologically. Sometimes Mrs. Kinney would just say "he isn't feeling well today" when Ernie would come by. Or, as they walked, he knew of hesitant, distressing moments for his friend. But their conversation did not touch it.

He let others know of his presence, whistling a great deal in the hallways—for two reasons: everyone knew the sound not only meant he was happy, but, more importantly, it said . . . "Here I am, step aside for me!" Whistling became his white cane.

When Dick became a senior he had twenty classmates, a strong bond among them. There was conversation about the war, about the occasional school dances, the six-man football games, and even classroom antics. But very little conversation about blindness. Gloria never discussed it; to bring it up would mean not accepting him as a part of the little school group.

His grades were excellent. "First in grades, first in seating," someone said. He always had a seat in the first row, to help in hearing. Perched there, one hand cocked behind his left ear. "I used to bend my ear forward till I noticed I was getting a cauliflower!"

"We wondered about his hearing—but you never brought up the subject. A guy like him—well, you just knew it wasn't right to dwell on his problems." That was the sentiment of his classmates. They knew the hearing aid, studied its presence, but, after all, some kids wore glasses, too. It came down to about the same thing.

In the car, perhaps to a movie, Dick knew where he was; the bridge in from Route 8 had certain bumps to identify it, and there was always the sewage plant at the north edge of town; you could always pick out that vicinity.

He took advantage of every teaching aid; the American Foundation for the Blind, for example, devised a pad on which a jagged line could be made by a special compass for geometry classes, illustrating circles and their properties. Very useful in getting the picture. You accepted these aids and were grateful for them; each helped, but inside his mind were more questions. What of a career? How would all the pieces fit together?

How long could the hearing aid bring the rustle of leaves to him, the voice of his mother, the message of the musician?

Gloria tried to teach him the two-step; despite the success, however little it was, he did not attempt the jitterbug. For the few record hops in the gym he was on hand, happy to be with Gloria, the majorette, the cheerleader—and one who had a particularly intriguing voice. A distinctive Welsh accent. It was the voice that gave the added meaning to him.

He had the dances and the games and the occasional rides out Main Street, past the Green Lantern restaurant, over the bridge, and up route 8 towards Canton where movies beckoned. Hobart Kinney's store, in a sense, dominated East Sparta; the three-story building not only provided the only skyline, but it was across the street from the town pump, focal point of gatherings. Bricks had been donated by the many nearby quarries in 1921; for the pump, a paramount fixture in the village square—except that it was not square. The pump, in the middle of a three-way intersection of streets, was a turret-like affair in which one might expect a Bobby-type directing traffic if he were in Great Britain—and if there were enough traffic to be concerned with such things. Some people, when given the name of East Sparta, say, "Oh, yes, that's the little town with the pump in the middle of the highway!"

Dick and Ernie spent much time in George Barrick's drugstore and soda fountain down the street. Barrick held forth warily eyeing the grade schoolers and high schoolers who flocked there for candy and a chance to read the comic books in the rack by the window. Maybe a drink, too. Sales were never great, but you could see the kids lined up at the rack as you walked by.

You wouldn't see that Kinney boy there, however; he'd be at the counter. There was nothing to be gained by standing at the magazine rack.

But he enjoyed the rides over the bridge, the highway from store, from home to bridge to movies. He knew the highway many years. It was the same highway that stretched now, many years later, for a thin man with piercing eyes and keen mind—and loving heart. A man coming to town to talk personally with this young, agile mind of his student.

Donald Hathaway found doors opening unceremoniously at a crossroads about a half-mile northeast of East Sparta. There was a garage and a·restaurant there and, across the highway on the road that angled to the village, a white farmhouse. The Nimishillen creek, more devious than Route 8, flowed by the village road. Along the highway a sign announced "East Sparta: No Solicitors or Peddlers Allowed."

Hathaway rode the bus on this day in 1949. A dusty ride accented by each bump of road, heightened by each farmhouse, punctuated by signs; yet with all the anticipation of the meeting there was something suspended, almost ethereal. He had not had a student so thoroughly capable, despite the number of blind he knew by correspondence.

Leaving the bus after a tedious ride, he was close now, excited to see what his "new Keats" looked like in person.

He paused, straightened his topcoat, checking creases, debating a long walk to the village as the driver had indicated. Standing slim, imperturbable, he surveyed the intersection. A pick-up truck was across the road, near the restaurant; facing up to the need, he mustered courage to hail the driver, Lester Young, for a lift.

"Kinneys? Sure, I know right where the house is. Everybody knows them." Hathaway wondered if they knew of the poetry of the blind man.

Flinging his suitcase upwards, Hathaway then climbed into the cab, finding himself next to a massive white sheep dog. It shed profusely. Hathaway's black coat was over a blue serge suit. He wore both impeccably.

Uneasy now, tense, he rode into town, over the bridge and the bumps, past the Green Lantern, down Main Street, and then a right turn to the Kinney house.

He wanted to rush up, start conversing, but the white hairs needed attention; he thanked Young, made no comment about the shedding, brushed as best he could, and then looked intensely toward the house. Dick was sitting on the front porch—at least he assumed it was Dick. Hathaway approached, went toward the first step, fulfillment of trip at hand.

"Hello!"

Dick's face did not change; he gave no acknowledgment whatever. Hathaway hesitated, perhaps this was not the right house—and yet Lester Young had spoken warmly of the family in the brief drive there, and, besides, how many other families in a village this size would have a blind member?

"This the Kinney house?" Louder this time, expecting an answer.

But there was no movement at all from the person

sitting on the porch chair. No swing of head, no response at all.

Once more he tried. "I'm Don Hathaway. Long ride from Chicago!"

He measured the words, nearly shouting them, watching the face; it was weird, as though the journey had placed him in some isolated wrinkle of time, a suspended moment in which nothing was comprehended. This *was* the village, this *was* the house. But what was the meaning of it?

He had written, cleared the time.

"Dick? I'm Don, from Hadley."

What was it?

And then, as he questioned, staring at the face of this young man, unmoving, as he took the step upward, moved toward the porch hesitantly, the moment was no longer suspended but as with water, rock, and air it was of time-lessness, teaching him, ripening in awesome meaning; as he stood motionless absorbing what he was coming to know.

For the first time, Don Hathaway, who had tutored Dick and consoled him, guided him, who had sensed his deep talent, had led this distant learning—became aware of him fully. He had come to meet him after all the letters and assignments and poems and criticisms—and for the first time Don Hathaway was struggling to the realization that Dick Kinney, his prize pupil, was not only blind, but that he was totally deaf as well.

Dick had never mentioned that fact to him in all their rich, meaningful correspondence.

As Hathaway stood there comprehending, his earlier shouts brought response; Mrs. Kinney appeared on the porch, starting to explain as well as greet. And so the conversation he had anticipated finally began, though not in any way planned.

It was lengthy, and a bit laborious. Don did not know the manual, but Dick had a Banks Pocket Brailler, a clever device about the size of a coffee saucer. Keys could be punched by Don spelling out words with the letters recorded in Braille on a roll of tape about the width of a forefinger—which was used to pick up the impressions.

And, fortunately, there was plenty of tape on hand. "We talked by the yard, you might say," recalls Dick. "I think when the afternoon was finished we had enough tape for another triumphal return parade for General MacArthur!"

Dick's voice was adequate for Don to understand; pronunciations were clear, pauses appropriate—only stresses and emphasized syllables seemed out of place on occasion. Their conversation ranged from home life to the activities of the Hadley School, the number of people there, Don's other students, and, of course, poetry. The conversation was eager, enthusiastic, not ended till long after dinner.

Among other topics Hathaway brought up the matter of continuing the college education; yes, he thought that someone of Dick's caliber could handle it despite the deprivations. This impressed Dick; here was the first person to suggest it seriously, openly. Six years now, six tedious years of groping for purpose. Hathaway's remarks, made on the endless roll of tape, may have made deeper impressions on the fingertips as they moved across, down the line of tape. He would remember the words long after the tape had been tossed in the wastebasket.

He could do it. He just knew he could. Now another person knew it as well.

RETURN

Roots planted by the visit of Don Hathaway led to visible growth in mid-1950 when Dick addressed a letter to Mr. Robert Barnett, Executive Director of the American Foundation for the Blind in New York. The letter raised questions about returning to campus—was any aid available for a deaf-blind person? What were prospects for a deaf-blind earning a college degree somehow? Had it been done?

It had, of course. Helen Keller was the first and best known person to complete formal schooling; her handicap had become known—loss of sight, hearing, speech—at age sixteen months, and the process of education was laborious, frightfully despairing. Yet, ultimately successful. Yes, it could be done.

And, to the east, at St. Johns University, it was that very year being done again by a young man who had gone through a time sequence of loss of sight and hearing similar to that of Dick Kinney. Robert Smithdas of Brooklyn was nearing completion of his degree requirements at St. Johns, sustained in measure by his own courage, resourcefulness, and the aid of the American Foundation for the Blind which, quartered in New York, was close to Smithdas, encouraging the close support. The boost was also financial, the AFB having acquired contributions in support of the Helen Keller fund, money going to the training and support of guide-companions during the campus years, as well as research into development of aids for the deaf-blind in communication.

Smithdas' career was destined to be one of service in the cause of the handicapped; he would later continue his training, earning the master's degree in Vocational Guidance and Rehabilitation of the Handicapped from New York University.

But Dick did not know all that Smithdas had achieved, nor of the possible financial assistance. He was soon to hear, however, from Sam Chermak, telling him of new scholarship funds. Smithdas would graduate in a year, Chermak wrote, and Dick could be next in line. Chermak knew the great desire Dick had and was close to him in the struggle for he, too, had lost both sight and hearing.

The correspondence was opening doors for Dick. The possibility existed for return to college! How great to major in English, take manualed notes from classes, and weave them into a career involving writing!

His letters to the American Foundation, to the Industrial Home for the Blind, and to the State Rehabilitation Services for the Blind were having effect. Barnett replied from the Foundation for the Blind that they were "very much interested" in his background, abilities, and sense of purpose. Yes, there was a scholarship in Helen Keller's name—perhaps as much as $1,000 might become available to him. It merited further attention.

In that same year, 1950, Don Hathaway wrote the Foundation in Dick's behalf, pointing out that Kinney was, in Hathaway's measure, a "gifted poet" with some fifty poems published since enrolling in the Hadley course. He called Dick "exceptionally likeable, a gracious young man with a fine mind and a quick sense of humor."

There were others who were impressed by the young man's endeavors. Annette Dinsmore, a teacher of deaf children for some time before going blind in her twenties, a social worker in welfare programs in the Philadelphia area, then a counselor for the American Foundation, visited Dick in 1950. Satisfied with his philosophical aims as well as his talents, she wrote Helen Keller directly, endorsing Dick for the scholarship and urging Miss Keller's support of his application.

"Any deaf-blind to succeed in college has to be outstanding," she admitted at the time. "Exceptional, in fact."

With reference to the scholarship funds available to assist, Helen Keller wrote affirming the excellence of Dick's motive and ingenuity; speaking of the funds to which she had contributed handsomely, she asked, "What nobler use can wealth be invested in than happiness of human beings?"

In November, 1950, Dick made a speech to the Gideon Society of Canton. Unknown to him at the time, the audience included one person with particular interest in the talk—and in how Dick presented it. Back in the room, unobtrusively sat Richard Wood of the Ohio Department of Public Welfare, one of those to whom Dick had outlined in lengthy letters reasons for his return to college. Several days after the talk, Wood wrote, "One of my reasons for wanting to attend your talk was because I expect to be in Columbus next week at which time I expect to meet with Mr. Robert Barnett, Executive Secretary of the AFB. At that time it is my hope that your case can be discussed more thoroughly, and as a result we will have a more definite idea as to what vocational plan to recommend to you."

Wood added that he had been deeply impressed with Dick's manner of presentation.

So, it was a time of movement, with interest, motivation, speculation moving towards fulfillment of what had, at last, become something more than a dream, a deep longing.

The rainbow coming into view.

It came into focus when the committee administering the Helen Keller Scholarship funds met in her home in the fall of 1950; Miss Keller "emphatically urged" Dick be given the chance. The group notified him that they had heartily endorsed his program—a $1,000 scholarship was his. Spurred, Dick began telling friends he would return to college in February, 1951, starting the second semester of the school year.

Miss Dinsmore continued her efforts for additional funds, recognizing the hesitancy of many persons to support the idea of a literary career for a deaf-blind person. "There appears to be some question in your mind," she wrote to one source, "as to the validity of literary pursuits, journalism, and public speaking as a goal. It is true that many people consider themselves potential writers who have limited ability along that line, but it is our feeling that Mr. Kinney has shown extraordinary talent and should be given the opportunity to develop this. If he can become a writer this would be a highly desirable profession for him."

She added, "We are basing our opinion not only upon the letters of recommendation, copies of which were sent you, but upon the letters, articles, and poems which we have received from Mr. Kinney himself."

Two primary issues were involved in all of the efforts for recognition: the feasibility of a deaf-blind person achieving success in college and the merits of a literary career of some sort. Both of these, in turn, were tied up in the question of funding. Mr. and Mrs. Kinney had some funds to draw on for continuing the education—but it was the tangential range of expense that required both the philosophical and financial support of welfare agencies. A guide-companion would have to be found, he would have to be paid by the hour throughout nearly three years of schooling. Textbooks could be Brailled by several charitable agencies, but Dick would need precampus training in a variety of personal matters, those of safety, of the classroom, of personal relationships.

Annette Dinsmore, writing to W. P. Gregg, Supervisor of Vocational Rehabilitating Service for the Blind in Ohio, reminded that "it has been demonstrated years ago by Helen Keller and recently by Robert Smithdas that it is possible for a deaf-blind person to complete the academic work without lowering standards." She mentioned meetings with the president of Mount Union who expressed interest in special arrangements. He would listen.

That was important, inasmuch as Dick had inquired at several other schools without this consideration. Expenses would be less at a state-supported school, range of companions wider; thus he had written Kent State University, an additional twenty-five miles north of Alliance. John Reed Spicer, Dean of the College of Liberal Arts, was not encouraging however. In February of 1951, when Dick had once thought he might be back on campus, Spicer wrote:

We do have a special interest in handicapped students. But as matters now stand we feel that we can be of more service indirectly rather than directly, by preparing teachers and clinicians to work with handicapped students in many schools rather than by gathering these students and working with them here.

To provide adequately for the college education of the deaf and the blind would require more in personnel and facilities than we presently afford. Hence we are not likely to be able to do much more toward the education of a blind or deaf student than any college would, and in some respects we can do less simply because we have less freedom to work with individual students than do some smaller institutions.

Spicer wrote that he personally admired the "spirit and ability" evident in Dick's letter, but the University simply could not accept his application.

The family looked back toward the small Mount Union campus where the president had said he would listen. The curriculum was suited for Dick, though he nourished hopes that more attention might be given his needs at Kent State, the more specialized school; what remained now was the liberal arts college where he had started—if, indeed, that school would have him.

Richard Wood was doing much to assist. He arranged the crucial meeting with the college. The American Foundation promised to have Miss Dinsmore on hand. Wood wrote, "It is my hope that as a result of this meeting a definite decision can be made concerning your future program."

Decision! His entire future was involved. The president had to be convinced!

William Burgess Ketcham had been a Methodist minister committed to church leadership, of stock typical of presidents of small colleges. He worked from a dark, roll top desk in a small, cluttered office in the same building where Dick had been interviewed a decade before; Ketcham had not been president then, however.

He was concerned. Was it right for the college to consider admitting Dick under his twin deprivations?

Miss Dinsmore urged that the college try. She was hopeful.

The Kinneys were anxious for their son to continue his education. They thought he could do the work, given the right kind of guide and companion.

But if he could not keep up, if the manual was not effective enough, if the events of the campus were too much for Dick, Dr. Ketcham wondered aloud, would it all have an adverse effect on Dick's later outlook on life?

But others had tried it.

Oh? How many?

Well, there was Helen Keller.

Of course. But she was different in so many ways.

Robert Smithdas. Annette Dinsmore was speaking now. Smithdas was graduating from St. Johns. Now that made *two* people who had been able to achieve it.

Dormitory life? Social life? Library? Eating? Contact with other students? Ketcham persisted, probing, wanting to be sure—if anyone could be sure. He didn't want the school to be sorry later if it failed Dick's purpose. He deeply wanted to protect Dick from any psychological harm which a premature entrance back to school might bring about.

With each comment, each question of Ketcham's, Hope Kinney's fingers worked rapidly in Dick's palm, sharing.

Hobart Kinney spoke then of his son's academic goals.

John Dalton of the State Welfare Department spoke of the confidence his office had; he could provide aid and was willing to experiment.

Mrs. Kinney admitted that Dick at one point did not think it would ever be possible to return, but he had been given new confidence through Mr. Hathaway.

Ketcham now: What does Hathaway know about these things?

Then he added, "Maybe school by correspondence is what Dick really should continue to have."

Annette Dinsmore again: but it was worth a *try*.

Someone reminded Dr. Ketcham that no academic degree program was possible through the Hadley School. Courses, yes, but no degree.

A half an hour had gone by. Everyone had spoken, cautiously, deliberate, but, being honest, nonetheless cautiously. For the conscientious church school president, reflecting back on a thousand other decisions in his career of guidance, the answer this time seemed as far away as ever.

But not everyone had spoken. At this point Dick Kinney touched his mother's arm, asked, "May I speak?" All turned to him, his voice breaking into their discussion. "Could I get in a few words, folks?"

Well, of course. What do you have to say?

He told them. Near the end of a statement of his goals he cocked his head directly at Dr. Ketcham and said, "I am choosing Mount Union. At one time I was not sure Mount was the best place to continue, but now I am. *I* am selecting *you*. And I *can* do the work!"

A smile appeared on Dr. Ketcham, lingered as he nodded, conceding that Dick, acting as his own attorney, had won the case. Yes, Ketcham said, I will recommend admission. Make your plans accordingly.

Dick had won. Perhaps Emerson, one of his literary stars, was on his mind: "What I must do is all that concerns me . . ."

Several days later John Dalton wrote, "May I congratulate you on the selling job you did at the conference at Mount Union? I am sure your statements there represented the difference between acceptance of your plan and if not rejection at least continued haggling . . ."

The scholarship a reality, campus admission completed, there remained some additional funding for a guide. A month later Dalton could write that this, too, was now taken care of. "It looks like it is really going to happen!" he told Dick. "I wouldn't have bet five cents on the possibility three months ago, but you can be assured that I am very much pleased with the arrangements as they stand at the present time." The vocational plan was a good blend of work of many agencies: among the six agencies which participated were the National Braille Press of Brooklyn, the Stark County Department of Welfare, and the Bureau of Vocational Rehabilitation. The State Rehabilitation Agency would pay $135 of the tuition; Mount Union would handle the rest. Rehabilitation Services would take care of room and board and certain books. They would, in addition, pay tuition, room, and board for a two-week training session for Dick and a guide-companion at the Brooklyn Industrial Home for the Blind —and pay an additional $75 monthly for the guide-companion's services during the initial return year at Mount Union.

The American Foundation for the Blind would take care of the room and board for the guide-companion at Mount Union. Travel to and from Brooklyn, clothing, and all personal needs would remain the Kinney family responsibility. They were, of course, delighted with the decisions and began interviewing, with the aid of the State Rehabilitation Agency, for a guide. Summer was at hand, classes would begin in September; it was a bright, promising time.

How do you go about finding someone who can become a white cane for you? An interpreter, a selector, a presenter among the range of philosophical encounters in the classroom and social opportunities outside? Few had had any experience, but after several interviews set up by the state following a public announcement of the need, they found a young man who had not intended to apply to any Ohio college. A native of Missouri, he had a special "plus" in this search: his girl friend, a fellow student at Drury College where he had completed one year of school, was blind. He knew Braille and was familiar with the special concerns of the blind.

The opportunity to work with a deaf-blind would be a particularly helpful experience for him.

Henry Daum's academic interests, however, were primarily in the field of science: he was aiming for a pre-med degree in undergraduate school. This difference in professional interests would later become a key factor in the dissolution of their companionship, but for now it was just another door opening wide for Dick, another step towards fulfillment of his dream.

In August Henry and Dick went to Brooklyn for special training. The Industrial Home for the Blind, an adjunct of the AFB, was noted primarily for its short courses for supervisors of sheltered workshops willing to employ deaf-blind people. In this capacity it had, however, capability to share valuable lessons with the two students. Among the persons involved was Robert Smithdas; a graduate student now, he was remaining with the IHB in a staff capacity.

"We saw each other nearly every evening," Smithdas recalls. "Dick already knew the manual alphabet, so there was no communication difficulty for us." Dick's mode of receiving the fingered messages was, Smithdas felt, a bit awkward; he worked with Dick to be more flexible. He wanted Dick to receive "overhand"—that is, allowing the configurations to come on both sides of the hand, palm if convenient, knuckle side if convenient. The sender would not have to position himself rigidly.

Not unlike those earlier days, walking to grade school, feeling the slight touch of Rosemary's arm guiding him without words, Dick was now being guided; and his guide was being given every insight regarding possible problems —traffic, hostility, lecture-taking, curiosity, the weather, meeting people. Questions of personal needs, study habits. At the end of two weeks they were both primed for campus.

September, 1951. Ten years before, Dick had left home, been a part of this campus until a terrifying day when the wall of silence rose higher than he could ascertain. Now, returning, he found the campus was little changed; he was undergoing more stress and change than it. There were no new dormitories, although rooming was at a premium; Korean war veterans were everywhere, enrollment was at an all-time high. Where once the girls outnumbered the fellows, it was reversed now. And vestiges of temporary housing for young families remained—it was called "White Hollow" when constructed immediately after World War II, because of the close white painted trailer homes clustered at the northwest edge of campus.

The mammoth task of getting texts—Renaissance poetry, sociological tomes, for instance—into Braille involved many agencies. The New York Guild for the Jewish Blind, for instance, helped with "English Prose and Poetry 1660-1680." The Cleveland Chapter of the American Red Cross helped with Swift and Arbuthnut. The New York Association for the Blind, asking for two or three months' time, said "we would like to do something for Richard Kinney." The Lighthouse in New York and the National Braille press assisted. In some of the older poetry the New

York Public Library for the Blind provided Brailled copy. There were many others.

Faculty welcomed Dick "back to the fold." The Ecklers were delighted, the Gunnells were gone, but there were newer faces to encourage—men like John Saffell in history, who had served on MacArthur's staff in the Far East. To Hathaway Dick wrote in December, "the American literature prof is really grand . . . She is trying to sell me Emerson on Self-Reliance . . . I hope she succeeds. I'm surprised to find how much more I am getting out of the courses than when I was here before."

The year slipped by profitably, grades continued at honor level, the only possible drawback the conflicting career interests of Dick and his guide. Late in that school year he wrote Annette Dinsmore, "The year has been a good one . . . with much learned and considerable progress made. The stimulating college environment is in itself an education, of which scholastic studies are but one facet. I'm sure one learns as much from the people one meets as from the books one reads."

John Wilson, another blind student, was of great help to Dick. He learned the manual within a few weeks, could communicate perhaps fifty to sixty words per minute. Henry Daum could do a little better, but whether Henry or John was in charge—or on occasion another fraternity brother tried his wits at the manual—there could be classroom problems. Professors with a steady stream of information would speak at 100 or 120 words per minute. Verbiage had to be eliminated, unnecessary words were a part of spoken communication but had no place with the manual.

Even with the best of manualers the process was running behind the lecturer. Problems result. For instance, suppose the professor came up with a good, solid humorous observation. The remark would get to Dick from five to ten seconds after the rest of the class heard it. Henry or John would start chuckling with Dick about the time everyone else had finished. Dick, knowing of this, tried to keep his laughter within himself.

He had known of related dilemmas before, in high school. One afternoon in physics lab back in East Sparta, the teacher, Louis Rice, stepped out of the room. In the experiments Dick was always the one who could explain the theory while others checked out the practice. On that afternoon things turned to a merry old time, much laughter and loud kidding—increasing until the time Rice stepped back into the room. Unfortunately, Dick was holding court at the moment, loudly proclaiming some absurd observation in the realm of physics with wild gestures and exuberant descriptions as well as a roundhouse series of exclamations. He continued as Rice stood in the doorway, frowning. Having paused too long in making his presence known, Rice decided to step back out of the room to reenter a bit later—after Mr. Kinney had been forewarned by his fellows!

At Mount Union Wilson was close and Daum helpful but too involved in studies not akin to Dick's. To Annette Dinsmore Dick wrote, "If his load proves too heavy he must be prepared to lighten ship or by cheerfully accepting my attendance of one or more classes with another manualist."

John Dalton, after talking with Dick in early summer, wrote Henry that the decision had been made to secure a different guide. This was done with "thankfulness many times for the hours you have devoted to his rehabilitation program." In response, Daum recognized that his own academic program would be better served on another campus. He expressed hope that the right person could be found to replace him.

Fortunately, the "right person" was on campus all the time.

Several weeks later Dalton wrote that Ron Smith was a "typical college sophomore," that his chief recommendations were personality and genuine respect for Dick's needs. Mr. and Mrs. Kinney drove to campus during the summer session, visited with Ron; he was there making up a course he had failed. Perhaps not the best recommendation! But Ron turned out to be quite flexible in ways Dick needed.

What counted most was the sense of knowing his role. He was to be a companion, not a leader; Dick an equal, not some phenomenon. Ron knew the manual, having picked it up from Henry during bull sessions. His fingers were agile, if not thin. A sturdily-built young man, he had turned down two football scholarships at larger schools, opting for Mount Union primarily for its small campus, closer approach. Now, with Dick, he found the courses in English were the important ones. Goateed Eric Eckler was department chairman: witty, urbane, given to much direct contact with students. Both professors, the Ecklers lived just a block from campus, opened their doors frequently to classes in English literature, Shakespeare, poetry. Mary Eckler was equally loved on campus. "She made Shakespeare stand up like a modern man," said Ron, "and I didn't even get credit for the course!"

Fraternity brothers found ways of identifying themselves to Dick—with personal touches. Joe Check, for instance, made the sign of a check mark on his shoulder; Ron used a thumb and forefinger on the shoulder. Some had a touch behind an ear, back of neck—and Paul Mutzig's signal was a forefinger on his knee. Dick knew all his close friends in such efficient manner. And he knew of the wild antics of his brothers, too.

Check was one who certainly took the deaf-blind brother as an equal (as Dick wanted it). Nothing so simple as short-sheeting him; no, the prank Joe had in mind was much more sophisticated. He plotted it carefully, roamed the shopping area for a used mannikin from one of the ladies' store windows, and brought it into the house. "For Dick," was all that he explained.

In what way? Several of the brethren expressed concern. "You've got to be 'specially careful with him."

Especially careful was right; especially alert to the ways in which the prank could come off! He knew what he was going to do. While Dick was away several evenings later, Joe and cohorts went to the room, placed the mannikin in Dick's bed, neatly arranged under the covers, waiting there for the moment when Dick would retire and discover the "body."

Great sport!

No one was concerned about "being seen" as Dick approached that night; they had the lights on for good measure, chortled loudly as Dick undressed, found the covers in the lower bunk (Ron Smith had the upper one), and crawled in.

Results were entirely predictable. Fumbling, Dick was surprised at the new form with him. "Hey!" he muttered as he pulled back, wondering. Did he have the right room? Was there a mistake? And what form was this? After some hesitation, he became bold, did the only thing he could do—it is touch, after all, that he had to depend on, the touch of Rosemary's arm, the touch of fingertips, the touch of raindrops on his head—reaching out for the form, interpreting it the only way he could: by feeling it slowly, until enough of the surface had been explored, be it human or otherwise—hopefully without a slap in the face! Then he finally realized what had been placed there.

After a few wisecrack asides—given freely, on the assumption that some fellows had been watching the entire episode, he removed the mannikin unceremoniously, crawled back, and found sleep. He was not to forget about the incident, however. Later, determining who it had been, he waited for his moment. It came about a month later when Joe returned from nearby Kent State University. He had, with other brothers, gone there to help celebrate the pinning of a Mount SAE to a KSU coed. It was in the early morning hours when Joe flopped in bed and dropped in quick, deep sleep.

"Delicious!" Dick's happiness was delightful when he was told of the situation. He asked to participate. "Hold on a minute, till I get back!"

He found his way to the bathroom, picked up a new tube of toothpaste, returned, and, ascertaining where Joe's sleeping form was—stretched out across the bed much like the mannikin had been in Dick's bunk earlier—he opened the toothpaste . . . and slowly squirted it all over Joe. Then the covers were pulled over the gooey form.

In the morning, after a full night of sleep and some tossing and turning, Joe awakened to realize the full impact of Dick's revenge.

"In retrospect," Smith says, "I'm sure that all the tricks were right. It was the best way to let Dick know he was entirely accepted, neither above nor below the level of activity in the house."

It might have been dangerous to get too close to the likes of the Kinney-Check funtimes. Paul Mutzig, who used the knee tap for identification with Dick, tells of such an incident.

"It was after one of their many battles. Dick had vowed

he'd get vengeance on Joe. In the dormitory room my bunk was first on the right, upper." On this particular evening Mutzig was near sleep in his bunk. "I remember the presence of or feeling that someone had come in and was standing near my face—being on a top bunk put anyone at the door at that level. Just then a volley of shots rang out and I backed up against the wall quickly. By this time everybody was awake and yelling. Shots had been fired into the air, but in the semidarkness, I could now see somebody with a gun in hand; then came the distinctive high falsetto voice—'You've had it Joe Check! You've had it!' "

It was Dick, with a cap pistol. Laughing, he turned away, and went out the doorway with everyone in a state of consternation.

But Dick was quite capable of making mistakes. He had gotten confused in the dorm, for Joe's bunk was on the left—Mutzig's on the right. Dick thought he was talking directly to the right person, but was mistaken. Mutzig tried to make this clear to Dick. Unfortunately, this was almost impossible; how could you shout your name to a deaf person? With shots ringing, Dick's laughing voice, how could you make him understand he had the wrong bunk? The signal? Mutzig's special mark to identify himself? Sure. But remember the signal was a touch on Dick's knee! Mutzig tried frantically to reach down, but the distance from the upper bunk was too great.

In making a final stab for the knee, he caught Dick on the rear; then heard Dick shout, "You're getting fresh, Joe!"

The incident went beyond the fraternity house—thanks to Dick's own forgetfulness. In class the next morning Ron Smith manualed the details to Dick during a history lecture. The prof was in the middle of a lengthy detail when laughter rang out; Dick could not contain himself this time when he got all the funny story. His own silent world didn't object, but the professor was nearly beside himself. There are, after all, advantages to the manual alphabet. It is silent, efficient—and very, very private!

Keene Bridgeman tells of Dick's ability to outdo the shenanigans of his friends in another way. On one occasion, as Dick sat on the sofa reading Braille in the fraternity living room, someone tied his shoelaces together—a fact which Dick did not discover until he stood up and started to walk. "He found out who had done the deed," recalls Bridgeman, "and the next afternoon while his antagonist was in class, Dick took several pairs of his shoes, tied them together, and took them downstairs to the large chandelier, crawled up a ladder, and hung them there."

Isolated in sight and sound, Dick was no separatist; and the same incentive that led him to argue for his own case to continue education moved in other ways as well. He would have opportunity to go around with Ron, or John Wilson, or any others who could identify themselves with him, but there were times when he wanted to fend for himself. He would experiment a bit; from the SAE house he'd put a coin in the telephone, dial the cab company number, wait a few seconds, then, assuming someone had picked up the receiver, give his name and address for pick-up. "If the call went through, fine; I'd be there on the steps and the driver would get out, come up to me, and assist me in getting in the car. If he never came by, I knew the number had been busy or that I had misdialed."

In a letter to Don Hathaway in October, 1953, he said, "My social front is humming this fall. Consider, for example, my realization that I can use the pay phone here at the house without help. The simple trick is to look in the coin cup after I hang up. If my dime comes back I know the line must have been busy. If it doesn't I assume the call went through. Thus I can phone for a cab entirely on my own . . . and can go wherever the spirit listeth—whenever it listeth!"

It might be Whitely's tavern several miles east of town, or Polinori's restaurant across town. "I'd have a little adventure of my own," he says triumphantly. "I'd have a beer and a hamburger—very inocuous but wild looking for me! The most important part of the adventure is that I wanted to do it on my own." To Hathaway he wrote, "The lure was not strong drink but hamburger with onions; that is to say, a strong sandwich!" Getting home again was just a matter of asking the taxi driver to call back for him at a prearranged time. "This is the first semester I've gone solo," he wrote. "I like it."

Sometimes the brothers would hear him using the phone and follow at a discreet distance. Some might drive to Polinori's, light-heartedly referred to by Dick in a letter to Don Hathaway as "a highly respected den of iniquity much favored by the local intelligentsia." They enjoyed watching his "night on the town." Certainly there was no need to be secretive about their presence—he'd never hear them anyway. Dick enjoyed the juke box there, many times they would watch him feed nickels into it, place his hands over the juke box, trying to pick up some of the vibrations, trying to sense the rhythm, if not the melody. At Whitely's they recall Dick feeding the juke box and, totally oblivious of the number of people around him or their conversation, he would sometimes begin to sing. His voice was sopranolike and the tune, frequently inharmonious!

In all of these experiences, the urge to be on his own dominated. Joe Check knew of many times when he and others would invite Dick to join them. "No, thanks," was the reply. Dick turned down the offer to ride along, join the crowd.

Later in the evening, as the fraternity members were around a table at Polinori's or Madsen's, in would come Dick, strolling along, head high, walking past them, on to the counter.

"He *knew* we were there—and watching him. It was his way of saying 'See? I can be your equal!' "

Bridgeman recalled Dick at a downtown restaurant, preferring to sit at a booth next to the jukebox, feeling something—how much?—of the rhythm even in the floor tiles. Bridgeman adds, "He probably enjoyed it more than I did listening to the full melody."

How much do we *enjoy* what is around us? How many really understand the melody inherent in—what shall we use?—the Golden Gate Bridge? How many ever get out of the car, feel the bridge moving gently in the wind swells, how many of us put our hands out to touch the cables, feel the bridge sing to us? Is there a difference between Dick Kinney at some small town restaurant moving his feet slowly to be by the jukebox, reaching out to touch the bright glass shield and Dick Kinney over the waters of the San Francisco Bay finding communion with the giant superstructure of the bridge?

Dick went to the basketball and football games, enjoyed Ron's manualing of specific action. Baseball as well. And he tried dating again.

Now how could that be? How could he even *ask* a girl for a date? And what would it ever mean to her?

An independent spirit, coupled with some extra touch of ingenuity opened the doors to dating—and to the courtesies of inquiry. Sure, he could have a fraternity brother make a call for him, but dating is not meant to be with a third party! Besides, he had it all figured out.

He went to his room, used the conventional typewriter, and began a letter in which he asked a particular coed for a date for a fraternity party coming up. In the letter he noted that the envelope would also contain two return postcards, pretyped in Braille on the message side. One, he said, would have (in Braille) dots for "yes," the other "no." If she would like to accept his invitation, would she please return the card on which he had Brailled "yes." If not, thank you anyway, and he'd appreciate knowing with return of the "no" card.

Oh, yes—he then Brailled both postcards, then took the conventional typewriter and wrote "yes" above the Brailled word on the appropriate card, "no" on the other. No need to worry in case she didn't know Braille!

In due time a card was returned. Fingers quickly flew across the dots. She had said "yes"!

How to communicate during a date?

Laborious—but good for the spelling! He put on the white glove on which was inked all the letters; the girl would tap them in sequence, spelling out the words of an abbreviated sentence.

Campus wags liked to comment on how frequently Dick would start holding hands whenever he dated!

He tried the movies a few times, but it was not too effective having a date try to indicate the action on screen. Fraternity parties were his favorites for dates.

He was an integral part of the campus scene, accepted by the others. President Ketcham knew, as did the others, there would be no "silent" college days for him! He was active, making his own kind of music on campus. It requires awareness of language and its potential not merely for informing or describing, but for intimately sharing emotion. And we all yearn to be sharers in whatever intelligence or beauty we can claim. Dick wrote of this in a poem which is one of his most accomplished:

LYRIC RELEASE

To feel the thought within the breast
Mount to the lips and sing,
As some shy bird within the nest
Should serenade the Spring;

To feel the small words, silver-bright,
Thrill up and cool the tongue:
No fountain, leaping to the light,
More joyously has sung.

For there's a yearning in the dust,
The rich, warm dust of man,
That will be silence if it must,
But music if it can.

He would make it music as often as he could through an active mind capable of deep academic insight, the pranks of an immature youngster, the solitary journeys to probe the length of his own shadow.

Paths of poetry take meandering routes. If one thinks of East Sparta, Ohio, as an unlikely place for a worldwide figure to be identified with, move a few miles—not more than 20—to a farm near the small town of Minerva. There an elderly, grizzle-bearded man with perpetual pipe in mouth slowly worked the fields of an adopted nation. Don Hathaway and Dick, visiting in the summer of 1953, traveled to his home, paying homage in one sense, eager to share poetry as well.

Many years before, Ralph Hodgson had written of the moors of England which he loved. As a critic once said, he was born to poetry. Now, a chance meeting in Japan leading to marriage to a missionary woman from the eastern hills of Ohio brought him here to farm, to live in quiet contemplation. In 1954 he was given the Gold Medal from Queen Elizabeth, awarded for works of former years. Few knew of him in the Minerva area until the National Institute of Arts and Letters gave him an award for "distinguished achievement to an eminent foreign poet living in America."

His poems were much of nature. He had written

> *No pitted toad behind a stone*
> *But hoards some secret grace;*
> *The meanest slug with midnight gone*
> *Has left a silver trace.*
>
> *No dullest eyes to beauty blind,*
> *Uplifted to the beast,*
> *But prove some kin with angel kind,*
> *Though lowliest and least.*

That is why, perhaps, he came to those remote hills, away from sophistications but close to the simplest expressions of nature. Such simple beauties appealed to Dick as well.

"Patience is required more than anything else," the lanky host said. "Even indifference more than painful working and working and working on poetry." He was probably the first man Dick had met who was wholly dedicated to poetry.

"Now, Mr. Kinney, will you read some of *your* poems?"

He spun a half-dozen of them, one in particular finding responsive chord. "Lyric Release is particularly effective. Yes, it's *very* good."

Eight years later the Englishman began to speak more of blindness as his own sight failed severely. Perhaps then he thought of the younger man in whose sightless, silent world had been the music of poetry. Shortly after that afternoon visit he wrote, "It has not been easy to read and study your poems without pitying reference to the sufferings you have undergone, and your unimaginable disabilities: I have striven to read them without that bias and have reached this conclusion: 'Lyric Release' will find its way into the Golden Treasury in proper time . . ."

Another "proper time" was upon him; he was finishing his college career, 126 credit hours on official transcripts. Four of those hours in physics earned a grade of B, two of them in Child Psychology another B, and Principles of Speech the final two hours of B. All of the rest—118 credit hours—were graded A, with an accumulated point index of 3.93. He would receive his degree in June of 1954 *summa cum laude*—"with highest honors."

His career as a writer-lecturer was still high in thought —something he could do on his own. Two years before he had written, "The American Literature prof . . . is trying to sell me on Emerson's Self-Reliance just now. I hope she succeeds." Those who sensed his leadership in many fields were setting many steps in motion. In December, 1953, Annette Dinsmore wrote to John Dalton that "it seems important to start planning for Dick's employment. It is my feeling that he should continue writing consistently in the hope that he can make a place for himself in the literary field—poetry and prose."

"Last summer I talked with Mr. Dorrance Nygaard, Director of the Hadley Correspondence School, suggesting that Dick conduct one or more courses in journalism and poetry for their correspondence students. Nygaard seemed favorably inclined to the idea as he is well acquainted with Dick's ability. . . . It would do no harm to follow this up. What would the possibility be for his obtaining

76

lecture work? As we both know, he is a delightful speaker."

Hope Kinney received a letter from someone in his audiences during that graduation year who observed, "Mr. Kinney read only two poems but they were so beautiful. His beautifully modulated voice and excellent presentation made it almost unbelievable to accept his blindness and deafness. He has not accepted it, and neither can we. We could not feel sorry for this superior gentleman." The writer concluded, "I could only feel sorry for myself and the rest of us. We have done so little to avail ourselves of life's opportunities and our own potentials."

He evidently had impressed Hadley officials similarly. With Don Hathaway in his corner, Annette Dinsmore and John Dalton encouraging, Dick received a telegram that the director of the Hadley School was coming to the Mount Union campus. Nygaard offered him a position with the English department. Dick wrote Hathaway at the close of his degree program in January, 1954:

"I don't know whether Mr. Nygaard has revealed all yet or not, so this may be confidential. In any case, the grand news is that I shall soon be paying Hadley a somewhat more extensive visit. In fact, I hope to stay forty years or so, a prospect which makes the past college years seem even more worthwhile. The thought that, having been so fortunate in my own education, I may now be able to help other handicapped persons improve theirs, is indeed a heartening one."

With the lecturing possibilities, doors were opening again for Dick, the reaching out of his own was returning once again. "All through college I've had the cooperation of so many people and agencies. So many wonderful guides."

In February he wrote Nygaard, "Preparations are in full

swing here for my change in habitat. For some reason I can't help thinking of Chicago as 'out west' and am laying in enough supplies for a covered-wagon trek. The Lord willing and creeks don't rise, we'll be seeing you soon."

When May came, after brief acquaintanceship with the working of the Hadley School, Dick was back on campus, a returning hero acknowledged officially now as class valedictorian, official spokesman for the class of 1954.

The college decked the narrow stage of Memorial Hall with potted ferns and palms; a purple banner was hung behind the stage, and temporary steps installed so that participating seniors and faculty could march down aisles, up to the stage, be seated by the lectern at Senior Chapel. An organ poured out tones reverberating as eyes turned, faculty in academic garb after a short, traditional walk across campus from Chapman Hall. Then came the seniors, as the rest of students and some five hundred townspeople and parents watched. Two seniors in particular were noticed, both going directly to the stage.

Ron Smith began manualing; then the last music faded, the invocation said, and they were seated.

There were 126 in the graduating class that year. Vince Obmann, class president, was on stage as well as Dr. William C. Wesley, acting president of the college, and Dr. John Saffell, class sponsor. President Ketcham had passed on a year before.

Dr. Saffell spoke on "The Simple Truth and the Single Virtue." Dr. Wesley announced a variety of prizes, Vince Obmann turned over the class gavel to the incoming president, and the ceremonies were like those of the school's tradition.

Then Dr. Wesley announced the valedictory address. Mr. Richard Kinney would speak. Smith manualed, Dick smiled, arose and, guided by Smith, reached the podium.

"Parting is not sweet sorrow," he began in a voice that searched, it seemed, for definition, ranging from alto to tenor. "In saying good-bye to our college days we are say-ing good-bye to a part of ourselves. We shall never be so young again, may never be so ambitious, or hopeful, or idealistic again. What parting can be more poignant than farewell to a portion of our youth?"

Annette Dinsmore was in the audience, Richard Dalton was there. Hope and Hobart Kinney, of course, had driven up. Rosemary and her husband were there. The press moved back and forth across the front of the auditorium, flash bulbs exploding in Dick's face; and those in the faculty section, in front of the audience, watched for the slightest reaction. There was none.

"Not that college years have been all moonlight and roses, bright hopes and far horizons. We came to college realizing that—but why did we come? What were we seeking? Only by answering questions such as these can we judge whether we have found what we sought."

Twelve years before he had stood on the stage of the East Sparta gymnaeium, valedictorian of the twenty-one member class. He saluted the past, at that time, spoke of the future, looking forward between lines to his college degree. It had taken much longer than he once hoped.

"The easy reply is that we come to further our educa-tion. But education is a relative word. To some, education means how to make a living. To others it means how to make a life *worth* living. Surely the latter aim should be the true goal of the liberal arts student."

Ron Smith was seated, listening. He had not heard the remarks before; Dick had rehearsed them for no one.

"We live in an age of specialists, each specialist an authority on six square feet of a continent of a thousand miles, each specialist calling on all other specialists to bear

79

witness that his own little plot of knowledge is the most important area in the universe. Our specialized civilization has turned life to jigsaw pieces—and we wonder why we cannot find a pattern!"

He read from Braille, fingers moving across the cards, his head always high, as though his eyes were right at you. In the faculty section someone shuffled feet, another tugged his robe hood. You notice these because of the overwhelming quiet.

"For life, after all, is a many-sided adventure requiring many-sided human beings. The glory of the liberal arts college is that it caters to the *whole* man in a fragmentary age. Especially is this true of a small liberal arts college such as Mount Union, where personal relationships remain more important than statistical averages."

By 1970 the senior chapel ceremonies would become object of ridicule by some students who, having no traditions, understood none. This day, however, the Hall was full, extra chairs in aisles.

"Here we have learned—or have been given the opportunity to learn—that knowledge, thought, the cultural heritage, are essentially human achievements meant to enrich the lives of living men and women. Here our classmates have not been merely classroom oracles, but individual guides. Specialize we subsequently may, but such specialization will be based on the broad foundation of a liberal education."

He is thirty-one years old, talking about youth and idealism and guides and fragmentation of thought. Listening, those who found intrigue in his voice, perhaps humor in its wavering quality, watched fingers moving and tried to imagine what it was to say these things in a void, not a pinprick of sound, not the slightest sliver of light.

"The proof as to how well we have achieved a liberal

education at Mount Union will not be found in point averages or academic records. Rather, it will lie in how we live hereafter. In how resourcefully we face the outer world with inner resources garnered on this campus. Problems can be opportunities for the flexible man; life, even in the hydrogen age, can be gracious for the truly educated man."

A man talks of graciousness in the age of the bomb. The faculty moves uneasily, hesitating on full acceptance and yet this graduate has said that problems—how many do *we* have?—are seen as opportunities. Have we pondered that?

"Our last word, then, is not the traditional Hail and Farewell, but a more challenging Farewell and Hail! Farewell to the yesterdays we have loved. Hail to the tomorrows that can be richer, fuller, more meaningful because Mount Union lives."

He stopped, head still high, hesitating slightly, then stepped back slowly, feeling for Ron's hand, touching. Ron moved around to the front, putting his hand on the chair—they had arranged it that way, not more than five feet from the lectern. Then he sat down, the speaker not aware that as he finished there had been silence and that silence had continued even as they watched Ron come up, watched the seating. Silence, ironically, was one element the speaker knew intimately.

Then from the bleachers the clapping began, swelling throughout the hall, crescendoing in a unified swell across the sea of hands. A faculty member arose, another, and a second wave was manifest as the audience arose, rushing to meet the thunder of their own clapping. More than a few of the faculty openly showed tears of rejoicing.

Ron Smith touched Dick's left palm, moved fingers.

Dick smiled. Ron manualed again, and Dick arose and bowed.

Coverage of his valedictory and graduation was nation-wide. *Time* magazine referred to him as "indomitable." *Newsweek* quoted his lines that "problems can be opportu-nities to the flexible man; life, even in the hydrogen age can be gracious for the truly educated man." The maga-zine spoke of the "bright mental imagery" of this man who had not seen for a quarter century. *Newsweek* later printed one of his poems to support this; "Vista," a simple poem of one brief image of the sunset. How many poets seek to capture the beauty and intrigue of sunset with awesome phrasings, sweeping generalizations! Not so for Dick, who crystallized sunset entirely in one image of a yellow car:

> *Day drives its yellow roadster*
> *down highways of the west*
> *'Til even the far red tail light*
> *fades on the dark hillcrest.*

Annette Dinsmore, on campus for graduation, brought Dick a chess set. Aware of the publicity attendant with the completion of his degree, she asked, "Is your head swell-ing?"

He paused briefly, then answered candidly, "Yes." Then he added, "But to just one-half the size of your heart."

Rosemary, living in Cambridge, Massachusetts, where her husband was in graduate school at Harvard, took note of the nationwide publicity that had come to her brother, only the third in history now to have earned a college degree while deaf-blind. "I'm going to start referring to myself as Dick Kinney's sister," she wrote to him. "Why not? Look at all the Kennedy girls who became known for the teas they held for their brothers!"

Bob Smithdas wrote, "How much more difficult it was for you than Helen Keller or myself to resume your studies as a deaf-blind person. Helen Keller and I have lived with deafness and blindness throughout early youth and were able to adjust and adapt to it long before we went to college, whereas you had to learn to live with deafness and blindness at an accelerated pace before you could think of returning to study at Mount Union College."

Nine years. An accelerated pace?

How would those of us who are "normal" know how to calculate the pace necessary?

Helen Keller wrote, "Proudly may I congratulate you on wresting victory's palm from limitation." She continued, "I rejoice even more because you show a free spirit in climbing to the hill-tops of song." Knowing of the role that poetry played in his life, she wrote, "It is wonderful to live above handicaps and thrill the air with melodious verse—a gift of the gods—that opens the mind to the glories of the universe."

Several days later "Dick Kinney Day" was celebrated at East Sparta with more accolades, including a message from President Eisenhower. The little town was basking in the achievement of its favorite son. His work now, however, was leading away from Ohio, his village, his campus, his family. Leading to the Hadley School, to Winnetka where he would continue to find purpose in his life. Westward to a suburban Chicago community of charm, a vastly different kind of village than he had known before.

It would hold for him, and for others yet to meet him, its own rainbow.

HADLEY

Through years of experience William A. Hadley had gained respect of students, both in teaching techniques and his own warm personality. In 1916 he looked forward to retirement from high school teaching, some plans for study abroad as well. None came to fruition, however, for that year, at the age of fifty-six, he became blind. A friend suggested he try broommaking, an activity—perhaps the only one—the blind were capable of handling. You could learn some menial task, nothing sophisticated, of course. The blind certainly shouldn't teach.

"But teaching has been my whole life," the man protested. Convinced that he could still play a useful role, he learned Braille and then pondered the possibilities—and need—for making more textbooks available in Braille. By 1920 he was thinking seriously of a "school" for the blind—in the front room of his home in Winnetka, Illinois. A school by correspondence. Dr. Edward V. L. Brown, the oculist who had given him the final verdict of blindness, endorsed the idea, pleading financial support: "I'll get the money if you can do the teaching."

Hadley advertised in the *Matilda Ziegler Magazine for the Blind* and had excellent results. Few of the blind had been reached by personal visitation; instruction by mail was a novel method of finding many whose lives were bleak. Hadley proposed a course in learning Braille by correspondence—and found many persons, in reply, urging courses in English, mathematics, and history, too.

The first student was a Kansas housewife who mastered Braille in seven months. In less than a year there were ninety students; by 1922 the school was incorporated as a nonprofit institution. The Kansas housewife paid no tuition; no other student did in all the years to come. Most blind were in bad straits financially; contributions would undergird the entire school program.

Alfred Allen was the first paid employee, serving as secretary, staying for several years as courses in Bible, English composition, and business were added. Later Allen became a field representative for the American Foundation for the Blind.

Other courses followed—expanding into twenty-one years of leadership by a man who once looked forward to retirement, a part of human life he never experienced. He once said that his life became worth much more after he had lost his sight, accomplishing so much with his fledgling school. Within three years some two hundred students were enrolled, the school firmly established.

When Hadley died in 1941 at the age of eighty-one, he had followed well a philosophy developed during the formative years of his school. He had written then, "When your life's ambition has failed you—pick up a new thread of endeavor. Make your renewal of effort count for other people and eliminate yourself entirely from gain."

It begins with this sense of renewal. Then it includes the practical steps, beginning with Braille, cells of dots, combinations for fingers to touch and minds to know. Today the Hadley School for the Blind remains the only correspondence school of its kind: "The University of Courage" was Hadley's favorite name for it. The range of courses became wide: piano tuners study arithmetic to help keep their records; newsstand operators study salesmanship; typists study spelling; a young minister at Harvard Divinity School studies Greek and Latin.

In Winnetka, Illinois. Suburb of Chicago, north shore. In early summer the red maples bend in gentle breezes that herald the dawn. Through the night from O'Hare Field jets today have coursed in wide arcs to the north-west, cutting slits of contrails in the darkness, their wail first angling sharply upwards, becoming flat whistles across the quilt of suburb. They come in atmospheric cadence, pendulum lines against the deepness of the night. Now, with this day they trail white cones as their whine blends with that of the Chicago and Northwestern diesels, green on cream, scooting along rails working southward, set in a trough that bisects the city.

Elm Street reaches on through to Lake Michigan. On soft mornings you almost hear surf reminding you of its presence and white gulls squeak like winged donkeys. Elm, where Tudor architecture dominates like some vin-tage square, gives an old world aura. Deep brown timbers against cream walls, plank texture against rippled stucco. Stores reminding one of alpine chalets line up, deep brown and white above, red brick and glass expanse below. On the corner, awning rolled up (for it is not yet time for bright Illinois sun which can bake crevices in the street) is the Sweet Shop.

Hip-roofed, the city hall south on Chestnut, with low wings suggests a mother hen fluttering her brood. On either side, beyond the lazy hump of Elm spanning the suburban tracks, are dormered homes, whites and grays on narrow clapboard sidings, then rail fences—some are raw poles left weathered, then again the white picket fence. Old timer trees, three times higher than homes, now like watchmen, now from afar webs of mottled brown and green.

But these sights and sounds were not part of Dick Kinney's introduction to Winnetka. His was, most of all the touch of the Hadley School. It consisted in 1954 of one suite of offices in the community house, the staff numbering six full-time. Dick's arrival prompted something of a celebration—and a time of learning the manual. All six did, although several relied on the white glove primarily. No one person was "assigned" to Dick; he was simply a member of a teaching team, talented enough to fulfill his own commitments. He got around in the rooms readily, having a floor plan on raised-line board. During daytime hours he worked with a steady flow of mail—Brailled assignments leading to evaluations and the writing of his additional insights and guidance with his own Braille typewriter.

Inasmuch as the blind of all ages utilized Hadley, he found himself dealing with junior high school English in some instances, with classical poetry at the college level in others. Again, it might be writing articles, personal experiences, perhaps simply writing correspondence. People improving themselves.

He had a room in nearby Wilmette with kitchen facilities. It was a temporary home; later he found an apartment across the street from the new Hadley building. The school provided transportation—and many invited him to their homes for dinner, conversation via white glove. His range of conversation delighted hosts—and perhaps this range was responsible as well for his concerns about some of the lesser assignments he had.

Evening programs promoting Hadley through better

understanding of the blind were of good purpose; they were not inspiring to him, however. "Work with students stimulated me, and I enjoyed the personal contact even more. However, for a while there I thought I was being used in programs as nothing more than a guinea pig."

He disliked being paraded around so that an audience could see how to guide a blind or deaf-blind person, and he disliked being thought of as some kind of freak. His own personality permeates this portion of a letter sent home, describing a typical evening "performance" for a woman's club:

Both Don and Ny were pleased by our first two programs. Ny seemed almost jubilant last evening on our way home. The Hadley program really isn't so much different from our own little talks before groups, Mother, the chief difference being a little more equipment. Here is the agenda for last night:

1. Introductory remarks. Ny.
2. The Hadley story. Ny.
3. Types of courses. Don.
4. How to guide a blind person. Ny and R.K.
5. Lightboard. R.K.
6. Dictionary. R.K.
7. Reader's Digest. R.K.
8. Models. Ny and Don.
9. Typical lesson and reply. R.K.
10. Poem and concluding remarks. R.K.

The program last night was at a church, about thirty women being present. As you see by the agenda, I have it easy till the fourth number, an item originally designated as "How to lead the blind." I told them that they could lead a horse to water, but they would have to guide me. There is really nothing to this except pointing out that the guide should give the blind person his arm rather than seize the victim's arm and start propelling.

The lightboard is simply a battery-powered lightboard with

six bulbs in the form of a Braille cell. I operate the keyboard to illustrate the alphabet, meanwhile ad libbing in what we hope is the Hope (Bob) manner. Ny prints an "L" on my shoulder when I get a laugh.

We take two volumes of the big dictionary to each program and invite someone in the audience to call for me to look up some word or other. This means more ad libbing while searching. Last night the word was "lift." My line went something like this: "Opening the dictionary at random we have— lumbago . . . Now we are at 'limp.' (Flipping the pages.) In pretty bad shape tonight, aren't we? You know, they call English the mother tongue, but Father Webster seems to have a pretty good vocabulary. (Flip, flip). At home I have what is officially known as a vest pocket Braille dictionary—only eight volumes . . . Ah! Here we are! We've got 'lift' cornered on this page somewhere. Presto! The word is defined . . .' (Reading). And so on. We got about five laughs on the dictionary last night.

For the Digest. Ny has someone in the audience open a Braille copy at random. I then find the beginning of the article. When I've read the title aloud, three people look it up in print copies and they and I take turns reading. How do I know how far they've read? I don't. I just keep on reading silently myself and begin aloud wherever I happen to be when the signal comes. Fearfully spontaneous! The Digest was the hit of the program last evening and entirely by accident—almost. The article was a thrilling one about a rescue at sea. Ny forgot to tell me to stop reading to myself the last time and covered it up by saying that I was interested in the article, a remark he passed on to me. I replied that, yes, I certainly was and would finish it after the program. Since this drew an "L," I continued to read during Ny's next speech. He went through the motions of flagging me down, after which I waited a moment, then began to read stealthily with one hand. He pushed my hand away, after which I closed the magazine— with my hand inside, still reading. I couldn't be sure all these monkeyshines were registering with the audience, of course, but was told later that the ladies loved it . . .

Dick wrote regularly to his family, sharing by typewriter the adventure opening to him. Whatever success in "lecturing" was coming to him, he knew Hope Kinney especially wanted to be there with him, know of every detail. He was still passing examinations, beyond the college degree.

He became a favorite around Winnetka quickly. His lettered glove a mark of special personality. The white glove, however, was not to keep its accustomed prominence among the "uneducated" for long. In New York, over a period of years, The American Foundation for the Blind had been quietly working to develop additional means of communication for the deaf-blind. Starting with awareness of the universality of Braille among the deaf-blind (thanks in great measure to men like William Hadley), engineers of the AFB laboratories had sought to provide a means of translating inkprint letters into Braille, sighted letter identification to nonsighted. Shortly after Dick began his work in Winnetka, an experimental model of such a "touch letter" machine was given to him for judgment.

In essence, it had a keyboard with letters arranged alphabetically; as these were pushed by the operator the pattern of Braille dots would form elsewhere on the machine, metal dots which could be touched by the fingers of the deaf-blind person. Seated across from the sender, this receiver had fingers placed so that he received the Brailled impression one letter at a time, not on a page or on a tape, but, rather, in a momentary thrust of dots on the fingertips.

When the mechanism was finally approved by their high

standards, the American Foundation gave it the name "Tellatouch." Today it remains one of the most liberating pieces of equipment for the deaf-blind.

Dick began carrying one around with him, a miniature typewriter some called it, an oversized purse said others. By whatever judgment, it became the primary means of the "normal" people talking with Dick. As Dick continued with Hadley he was called on for television appearances, radio talk shows, more and more. He called Tellatouch "invaluable," its speed nearing that of the pace of an expert manualist.

Betty and Robert Oakes Jordan were among the closest of Dick's friends at Hadley. An electronics engineer, Jordan would later (in conjunction with his work for Illinois Bell Telephone) perfect the Tact-o-phone, a device for transmitting Morse code via telephone to give further assistance for the deaf-blind. Until that device was perfected, however, Dick Kinney was learning to devise his own amateur solutions to the variety of seeming obstacles confronting a person living alone without sight and hearing. He found he could use the telephone even more than he did at Mount Union, calling a cab for a trip to Polinori's or Whitely's. With a private phone, he had no need for nickels and dimes for toll calls—but, then, he couldn't check for coin return in case the call didn't go through. He had his own new solutions this time.

He found that by pressing the earpiece to his palm he could feel the busy signal beat like a pulse. If he did not feel it, he assumed the other party was on the line, waiting for Dick to speak. He also clued in those whom he called frequently for a system of clicks to give short answers—one click for "yes," two for "no," three for "I don't know." Dick could not hear those clicks—but they did register by pulsation against his palm again.

If there should be question about the answer, Dick would then ask the person to call back immediately—the vibration of the ring would confirm that Dick's call had gone through, his message understood.

With Tellatouch under his arm, Dick learned that he could go by taxi quite freely, once his call got through. He went to the airport alone and once went into downtown Chicago, met a sighted pen pal, dined at the Italian Village, went shopping in Chinatown, and returned to Winnetka by taxi. The Tellatouch meant the difference. However, it was imperative that Dick have someone "with" him who would be a guide in traffic. The blind have an echo perception which can pick out distances by the sound of noises against walls, streets, cars. Not so for the deaf-blind. In such expeditions he was dependent upon the goodwill of those around him, who heard his voice, heard it explain the Tellatouch operation, and who followed his instructions. He was blazing his own trail, but it would never be an isolated one. The way, the thought, the good was "wholly strange and new," but it was isolated only in sound and sight, never in mind or humanity.

In 1956 he found the apartment which would be his through the rest of his bachelor days. To his parents he wrote, "We have found an apartment that looks very likely. Just two hundred feet from the Hadley lot where the new building will rise. The Sweet Shop is in the same block, just a few doors away. A barbershop is even handier."

The apartment was on the third floor of the Tudor-style building at 723 Elm at the corner where Arbor Vitae Street carries its Dutch colonials up a gentle slope. Upper floors in variegated rust brick, dark beam trim, then around the corner—where his windows were—the level becomes lighter, a stucco. Below, forsythia bursts, and branches play with light winds. The windows across the east face of the building were in pairs, those in the middle of his apartment. From out of them you could see the lot where the school of William Hadley would rise. Some could see that.

The apartment owner was not hesitant to rent it to a deaf-blind; some time before Mr. and Mrs. Franklin Deane, both of them blind, had lived in the same building, though not the same apartment. Further it was pointed out that Mr. Boal, the owner, had a brother who was on the Board of Trustees at Hadley.

Dick looked forward to having Rosemary and her husband visit with him as well as having some of the Hadley staff over for chess in the evening. His first out of town visitors, however, were his parents who drove to Winnetka to share in the celebration of the apartment.

Dick was proud to show off his independence: cooking by electricity, using an automatic egg-cooker, pop-up toaster (that way he could tell when the toast was right). He put his garbage in the back stairway can, set boxes outside his door for the maintenance man to take away, availed himself of laundry service and dry cleaning pick-up and delivery. The grocer delivered (use the telephone, give them the order, ask the grocer to call back to confirm having gotten the call, then keep your fingers near the bell to feel the pulsation).

At the school he found a kindred spirit in Marcia Berman, young library assistant who also handled orders when not shuffling the bulky Brailled volumes on sturdy metal shelving. She was intrigued with him from the very first day when she volunteered to walk him back to his apartment. Later, when it became apparent that Dick's work load and variety of personal appearances and speeches necessitated a special guide-companion, he asked that she be the one designated to assist him.

Marcia Berman understood. It may be that her own awareness of some taboos that society encourages was just what was needed to give that extra outreach in the case of the deaf-blind's need for touch. Her fingers moved smoothly over his palm, transmitting not only words but a kind of gentleness. Today Marcia talks about her long association with Dick in almost a flood of assertions. "I think the deaf-blind are more willing and anxious to communicate than the so-called normal persons. With them 'reaching out' literally is such a fundamentally right action. But the rest of us hold back, we think we're not supposed to hold hands, touch, stroke fingers across another person's unless we have some special relationship with them."

Dick recognized the need for others to be with him. "There was no need to be a hero," he said and once told Marcia that the primary reason he enjoyed having her walk him home after a day of work at Hadley was the fact that he just didn't want to get killed.

"I was a travel companion," said Marcia. "His walk was brisk, his delight in striding along very genuine—but he had absolutely no awareness of traffic. He could sense curbs and streets, but not traffic."

How, then, his solitary excursions to Chicago? His reliance was on the cab driver to deposit him precisely where he was to be, then on his friend (who was sighted, remember) to be there at that time to take up the guidance. The risk was in the timing, and in the integrity of the taxi driver.

Marcia became Dick's first secretary three years after his arrival on the staff. She did not have this as a vocational goal, but liked the job very much. "OK, maybe I was a secretary in a sense." She has something to say about terms: "I'd prefer the term 'interpreter' to secretary."

That is a better term. More than a desk assistant, she assisted him in travel to other cities for meetings in behalf of the blind and deaf-blind, in sessions for fund raising, for Dick was slowly moving into the realm of public relations. When he needed his environment interpreted, she was there.

But his twin "inconveniences" created awe in others, if not in Marcia. For example, Dick continued to be placed in contact with celebrities of all manner, paraded around the room to identify objects, turn on command. He was the dramatic symbol of the school, the one to be paraded before the dignitaries to impress them with talents and dominions. But Robert Frost, among other dignitaries, had difficulty responding. A meeting with Frost was arranged in one of the Chicago hotels; Hathaway, Nygaard, and Dick met him, Dick expecting a delightfully profound discussion. However, after Hathaway conveyed the introductions, Dick having acknowledged his presence, hand held out, Frost became very uneasy, hesitant. He pushed his hand through his mop of hair, said, "Ah, I'm, ah, very pleased to meet you." He then stared, almost transfixed, at Dick. Attempts at conversation failed, and the "meeting" concluded in a brief acknowledgment of achievements mutually accorded, Frost speaking quite low. To the others he spoke more freely—but of himself, uneasy, as though he were trying to fulfill a role.

Frost had seen the folly of men's walls, the simple triumph of hill folk, the strangeness of a brook flowing westward, and the awesome finalities of both fire and ice, but he had not encountered one before who could know of his presence only by touch. Relating was difficult.

"Initial communications," according to Marcia, "are

most significant. If you can get the conversation *started* with the deaf-blind it will move along." But the presence of the interpreter, the deft fingers of the manual or the mechanism of the Tellatouch can create barriers in some minds.

Back at the Elm Street apartment, the initial contacts with Dick were even more mechanical. Suppose you want to see him. You climb the stairs (Dick could use an elevator in the building, his soft knees since childhood restricting some ease of movement), go to his door, and knock.

Now, what good would that do?

So you ring the doorbell with equally futile results.

How can "touch" be derived from a doorbell? Dick came up with the answer.

He called it "fanfare" and said that it was the one doorbell system by which a friend who wants to drop by and shoot the breeze actually would drop by—and "shoot the breeze"! Oscillating fans, one in each room, were actuated by the doorbell button, and he could detect their operation, signaling someone at the door. Robert Jordan made the hookup for him. Of "fanfare," Dick wrote in *New Outlook for the Blind* magazine, "It has one pronounced advantage over an ordinary doorbell. Since the button must be held down for twenty to thirty seconds while the fans build up speed, friends know how to reach me, but the bill collectors don't!"

As in so many other aspects of his life, he was showing others lessons in a positive, uplifting approach to the problems surrounding him. His philosophy has been quite manifest: use your energies, such as you have, to work to change for the better those things that can be changed, accept serenely those that cannot. It gives, in Dick's mind, "the sense of responding positively to every situation. Instead of feeling helpless, one decides whether to endeavor to change the situation or to accept it serenely. Well, as serenely as possible!" Some aspects he could never change. He doesn't have the options that other people do in ordinary walk and conversation—he cannot, for example, rise and leave a dull party on his own; if he would like to window shop at Christmastime a bit, he cannot merely leave the apartment and catch the clear faces of the shoppers, drink in the panorama of festive store windows. Such limitations were not binding, however, on calling a taxi, having friends over for dinner, conversing via Tellatouch —or touching the singing cables of the Golden Gate Bridge.

The world of the individual mind. Every positive change or serene acceptance coming through his own intellectual identity. The extreme terror which any deaf-blind person can experience is that of losing one's mind, his memory, recollection, power of analysis, logical thought. For him there is no amusing show put on by others to entertain; it comes from within his own rational thought; to lose such process would be oblivion. With it there would always be the options of positive thought that he had spoken of.

Six agencies had helped Dick Kinney in his return to the Mount Union College campus for his degree; three deaf-blind persons had now achieved higher education, all three becoming national figures. There was a worldwide recognition coming to all of them as well—and a global effort in genesis for assisting the uncounted other similarly "inconvenienced." The World Council for the Welfare for the Blind in the year that Dick was graduated initiated first steps for consideration of the global deafblind. He was getting in on the ground floor. In Chicago in 1957 the American Association of Workers for the Blind held a special forum on communications for the deaf-blind at which time both Bob Smithdas and Dick Kinney spoke. Considerations of an international manual alphabet were made. However, much more fundamental effort and support within each nation was needed. Dick discussed the Tellatouch, offered several personal experiences which showed the achievement possible in daily social contact; Smithdas discussed the manual.

Following the meeting, in July, 1957, Dick traveled to Brooklyn for a United Nations committee session which had just undertaken study of the problem of the deaf-blind; his own outreach had begun to be global.

President Eisenhower recognized the significance of these early U.N. studies by inviting participants to the White House—providing Dick an opportunity to give him a copy of his booklet of poems. The Tellatouch was discussed as well, the President typing with considerable skill.

Having conversed with the President, he could look forward to other international figures—and a trip to Rome two years after the Chicago meeting, there to address the World Council on Welfare for the Blind. In what was called the "second most important speech of my lifetime," Dick addressed himself to the dilemma of loneliness for the deaf-blind. Poignantly, he answered his own rhetorical questions to bring home the point of what it was all about:

"Is it being snowbound alone in an icy mountain cabin on a winter night while the wind shrieks outside? Is it drifting alone in an open boat on an empty sea, with only the moon and stars for company? No, true loneliness is neither of these. True loneliness is sitting in a warm comfortable room filled with talking, laughing people and feeling yourself cut off—absolutely cut off—from all that friendliness and companionship because you are deaf and blind and not one person in the room knows how to communicate with you."

He alluded to the needed studies of both numbers and circumstances of the deaf-blind throughout the world. "How many families are waiting to be shown how to bring a deaf-blind son or daughter, husband or wife, back into the fellowship of the family circle? We do not know, but the number must rank in the tens or hundreds of thousands."

He would be returning to that theme in years to come; deaf-blind know no national or ethnic bounds.

Back at Hadley he was given additional duties—that decision made, in part, to his own tenacity in seizing opportunities. He heard that the school was looking around for someone to head the fund raising aspects of its program, no small task for as the new building arose and more and more students applied for the school's services, staff had to be added, equipment, researchers, all of which took considerable funding, for every service of the school was totally without tuition. Clarence "Bud" Jones, president of the Hadley Board of Trustees from 1952 to 1969, recalls that Dick was very anxious to undertake the new fund raising responsibilities. He made formal application. "But we'd never had anyone deaf and blind at the school before; at the time we were all convinced that no one with these handicaps could ever assume financial leadership." Logic was convincing; Dick was turned down and another person hired.

Several years later, when the opening developed again Dick had another chance. He loved teaching, had no intention of dropping it completely, but he relished the new, added responsibilities. Jones admits that it was his eagerness, his enthusiasm, an unbounding one, that turned the tide. "We concluded we just couldn't get anyone better qualified."

In 1958 he was named Assistant Director to the school, second in command only to Don Hathaway who had become Director following Don Nygaard's passing. In the capacity of Assistant, he reported directly to the Board, advised on curricular matters, assumed charge of any additional professional activities to "further the welfare of people who are blind," supervised all fund raising, including mailings, promotions, community chests, the Women's Board at Hadley, contact with church and civic groups—and was in charge of all publicity of the school.

He assumed the teaching of poetry writing; Hathaway's duties as director now forced him to drop all teaching. Dick thrived on the additional work. Marcia Berman's duties were coordinated with Merry Leary's, who was Dick's "afternoon secretary," Marcia being the "morning secretary" officially.

Mr. and Mrs. Henry Geiser, who lived in the adjacent apartment, took a parental interest in Dick which probably reflected some of their concerns for his well-being. And they had some justification for those concerns. On one occasion Dick had gone to work in the morning unaware that he had left water running in the bathroom. How many of us do that sort of thing even though we have ears to hear the sound? In Dick's case, he must conclude all bathroom activities with a check list, and on this morning he had neglected the water. The Geisers could hear it running, and recognizing that Dick was not in the apartment at that hour of the day, they notified the building janitor who got in to turn it off—then gave the Geisers a key in case of any other instance of similar emergency.

A different kind of experience came from his early-morning songfest in the shower. Apartment walls being something less than impregnable, shouts or songs would penetrate readily—especially if the singer had little idea of his volume! He enjoyed singing but the Geisers—who heard every tune—had to admit the melody was something less than skilled!

In the apartment he continued to enterprise solutions to the multitude of dilemmas confronting him in routine kitchen work, work preparation, and social contacts. He eventually got the services of a maid to come in to check the apartment weekly; till that time, however, chaos could occur—and occasionally did. On one occasion, working in the tiny kitchen, Dick moved a bit too fast from refrigerator to stove, in the process unceremoniously dumping a full casserole he had prepared. He was aware that he had knocked it off the counter—and that it probably had spilled over a wide area. What he could not know was the exact extent of the mess, and how much of it needed immediate cleaning. The supper, so well planned, was a loss, of course. But more important was the picture others might have of the situation!

He wasn't sure where the unfortunate casserole had landed—for him there was no sound of its hitting the floor —but it wasn't where it should be, and he had felt the brisk touch of it as he moved past the counter—a touch which signaled disaster.

Well, problems are opportunities and all that. He'd just have to face up to them. And to this one. He had on a white shirt from the office, a tie, and his suit pants. He knew all of these by coded Braille notes in the lining, same as his mother had provided through the years at home. To get to his knees in search of the debris would mean getting his good clothes dirty—after all, it would take two or three searches before locating everything. How much of a mess was there?

How could he be sure?

Strategy came after an extended pause. He moved cautiously across the floor—no need to *slip* in the casserole —got to the bedroom, took off his pants, laid them across the bed, removed his shirt and tie as well, then reached into his dresser. Down through miscellaneous socks, underwear, past a towel and then to—yes, there it was. He put on his bathing suit and returned to the kitchen, ready now for mop-up detail!

Clad in beach wear, he set about with bucket, dishrag, serving spoon. It took a long time.

Within a few days he had made arrangements for a maid to stop by to do all household cleaning.

She probably never saw him in a bathing suit.

Others saw him in more conventional attire. In 1958, for instance, pianist George Shearing, blind, who had known of Hadley School, was told that Dick Kinney was in his audience during one of his shows at the London House in Chicago. Shearing went to the microphone, told the audience that "a celebrity in his own rights" was there, then invited him to come on stage, up to the piano. Shearing then played a couple of particularly rhythmical selections with Dick "feeling" the melody by placing his hands on the piano.

Just as he had with the jukebox in years before.

Their friendship became very close, Shearing endorsing many Hadley fund-raising campaigns. In addition, Shearing later took several Hadley courses including one in business practice.

It was that same sense of touch at the piano that spurred Robert Oakes Jordan to perfect the Tact-o-phone in the Illinois Bell laboratories; the device transmitted Morse code with provision for Dick to place his finger over a special diaphragm. The dash was made by dialing 4, the dot by dialing 1, the length of time of the return dial established the "length" of the dash or dot. Jordan turned over all of the techniques learned from his experiments to Illinois Bell. An experiment sending a pine odor into the room when the doorbell was activated was another of Jordan's enterprises.

A variation of the Tact-o-phone was developed in Holland several years later. Dr. Gerrit van der Mey, a deaf-blind mathematician for the Netherlands Postal Telephone and Telegraph Service, devised it in conjunction with a colleague, Dr. William L. van der Poel. In this system, the person who knows the approximate time of a call anticipates its arrival by feeling special vibrations in a "feeling box." Impulses sent over the telephone lines are tapped on a machine similar to a typewriter and "demodulated" in a receiver box to activate the six pins of the Braille system. Once the message is received in this fashion the listener can reply, of course, with his own voice if the sender is not deaf.

Demonstrated originally at the Industrial Home for the Blind in Brooklyn in 1957, this device has had many variations since then. The Tellatouch, however, remained for Dick—and for most other deaf-blind—the best means of person-to-person communication.

They all add up to touch.

And a large dose of dominion.

It takes a measure of patience for him to use the Tellatouch for all of its opportunities.

Put yourself in his place; on your forefinger come the dot thrusts "H"-"E"—OK so far?—then an "L" and then another "L." You've got "hell" and it doesn't fit into the scheme of the sentence as you're getting it in your mind. Of course not, the person on the other end meant "he'll" but, built for compactness, the Tellatouch does not include an apostrophe key. Contractions can be dangerous!

Julie Finley, graduate of the Moser Secretarial School in Chicago, served next as Dick's "interpreter," then came Cathy Jackson, a student at Lake Forest College. Barely eighteen years old at the time, she was interviewed, as were all others, directly by Dick. She figured she "had to put forth" to show him she was capable beyond her years. "I put in a lot of 'damns' and 'hells' in the manual conversation—you know, like that was what a man expected in his language."

She found out differently. She found out that all she needed to do was be herself. He had selected her, as he had others, for her smoothness in conversation, not for the earthiness in it. That natural smoothness was a clue to her disposition—and Dick was good at clues. Some six years after graduation, he sat at his desk one morning reading some Brailled material, when he felt a touch on his shoulder. The thumb and forefinger it was, on the right shoulder.

He hesitated. Unsure of the mark, and yet it was distinctively thumb and forefinger on the shoulder.

Then, he remembered, "Ron! Ron Smith!"

Bridging years with the touch of a finger. You can symbolize just about all of what dominion means with such a reference—or perhaps it can be done with bricks and mortar which were rising in 1957, reaching completion in December of that year at 700 Elm Street. After 36 years of service, first from an upstairs bedroom study, through rented offices, the Hadley School came home to its own structure, a two-story buff brick building geared to special library, recording, office, and conference opportunities. It was financed entirely by contributions, much from the Winnetka area—the town considers the school its own child. When one looks at it today, since enlarged, nearly doubled in facility, worth at least $500,000, he is tempted to think that classes are held in the building; its size indicates this. But the work remains entirely by correspondence. Accepting this, you stare at the somewhat functional architecture, rows of windows (picture type with small casements on either side), imagine staffers in return staring outside at the changing panorama of skies, cars, houses, and then you are reminded that most of those on duty are blind. You look back at the windows, bemuse yourself over the large window that spans the stairway dominating the facade, and becoming aware of the simple architecture of that window—six large panels—you realize that those six panels are in the same relationship as the six basic cells of the Braille dot system.

The design was unintentional, but you feel that Louis Braille would not mind that aspect; the window itself remains mute testimony to everything the school and its history of service means. Perhaps it is right that the window design was unintentional; no need to parade blindness. Those who climb the tree one branch at a time do it without fanfare.

A hundred years before Dick Kinney was born, young Louis Braille sat on the stone step of his father's harness shop in Coupvray, France, making pinpricks in sheets of paper on his lap. He had spent all of his spare time that summer in this seemingly insignificant activity; passersby would joke at his labors, others would inquire solicitously but without full understanding of what the young man was so close to achieving. Blind since the age of three, he was groping for some means of communication so that the blinded could *read*. A basic six-dot series of pinpricks was the start; the months unfolded a system of dot patterns each identified with letters and punctuation marks.

He had read the few books available to him—with letters raised in full configuration; so bulky and impractical that only a few copies of books were available. And that meager supply had been exhausted many years before, when he entered the Royal Institution for the Blind in 1819.

The sense of touch—Dick Kinney once said "That's all that I have left"—held the clue for a new system of communication. By the time Braille returned to classes in the fall of 1823, he had perfected a system, the six dots, two rows of three each. It worked.

Six dots. Punched onto paper, a kind of embossing with enough variations to spell out an alphabet and enumerate all the numbers and bring a lifetime of reading and communication to the blind. Louis Braille was a three-year-old when he accidentally punctured his eye with an awl; infection spread blinding the other eye as well. Ironically, it was a deliberate use of the awl which he employed in punching out the first primitive dots.

The system worked beautifully, too well in fact for those who were the "leaders" of the blind at that time. With it the blind could scan enough of the world's messages, become their *own* teachers, maybe run their own schools. Why, if the blind became independent they would deprive the sighted of some of *their* jobs! Strange the vagaries of the sense of preservation in humanity!

At the Paris Institute for the Blind a decree was made finally that all use of Louis Braille's system was banned, existing materials were burned, anyone caught using the alphabet would be punished.

Other personalities, wisely, intervened eventually. It is a heartening footnote to the account that the very practicality of the Braille system would in the end insure its acceptance.

At Hadley, student enrollment in 1958 reached 1,287 including 177 from other lands. Four courses were given with full college credit, others ranged from poultry raising, sixth grade spelling, and fifth grade arithmetic to Esperanto, physical geography, and home economics. In all, 77 free courses for the blind.

Moving up in responsibility, Dick continued teaching and offering guidance to his students. To Eileen, a homebound girl whose legs forced her to a wheelchair existence along with blindness, he gave courage and hope when she heard about Hadley, corresponded, and sent in her first lesson in English. He wrote:

"By completing your first English theme within an hour after delivery of the Braille typewriter we were happy to lend you, an Irish colleen has proved again that to begin is half done. You have a large green 'A' on Lesson One."

He added, and you can almost see the twinkle in his eye as he did it, "You also have a special opportunity to improve your spelling of 'occur' and 'radar' . . . Sunshine and shamrocks till next time!"

A young girl manifested suicidal tendencies, which Dick noted in course correspondence; another student, an elderly man, had just lost his sight, reacted similarly. Terror long smoldering in one instance, frightfully sudden, final in the other. A flow of Brailled letters from Kinney helped prevent the suicides.

As he assumed more administrative leadership he attended trustee meetings and began to exert greater influence. One trustee remarked that Dick was the most alert of them all. "He was the only one who could have slept, and we never would have known it."

By 1960 he had accumulated enough evidence to indicate that of the some five thousand deaf-blind in the United States only a handful could really be qualified to teach other deaf-blind. Welling up within his thought was the necessity for more outreach by better preparing the deaf-blind to lead themselves. More teachers, deaf-blind themselves, were needed.

His global efforts to find deaf-blind who could help others had begun at Rome, with the meeting of the World Council for the Welfare of the Blind. He served as an official representative from the United States, nominated by Peter Salmon of the Industrial Home for the Blind; his work to teach the manual to the deaf-blind in other countries as a start to self-sufficiency. On this trip Hope Kinney accompanied him. It was a particularly significant appearance for him, his first global capacity, his message to the forty-nine-nation assembly, and the fact that he would attempt Italian language. He had never heard any Italian, never knew how he was doing with it, but felt determined—remember John Kennedy in Berlin—to use the language of his hosts to dramatize the bond among participants. Pronunciation hints were given to him in Braille by Italian students.

His message was primarily an inspirational one, a deaf-blind giving a plea for recognition of the virtues of the deaf-blind around the world. "Ours is a mission to show the world that to *know* is more important than to see; that to *understand* is more important than to *hear;* that to serve is truly to live."

Methods of overcoming grave limitations of the deaf-blind were stressed by him as he urged delegates to make the methods—the manual, the Tellatouch—more widely known to the deaf-blind and their families.

While in Rome he met with two other blind students in Florence whom he had known as pupils through correspondence. Later he had an audience with Pope John XXIII.

When he returned, the Chicago *Sun-Times* wrote editorially of him as "a bold crusader returned from a mission more awesome in reality than the exploits of many a mythical hero."

His "missions" were of diverse natures. It took no more courage on his part to cross the globe to preach the gospel of governmental interest in the cause of the blind and deaf-blind than it did to visit corporate offices in New York soliciting private gifts for the Hadley School. In both cases he was blazing totally new trails for the deaf-blind by doing the work himself.

Yet there was a psychological factor which may have aided him, especially in those trips to the corporations. His travel associates revel in telling how he would go boldly into New York offices, never affected in any way by plush surroundings, the trappings of the mystically wealthy. "It never impressed him because to him all people were alike, wealth could only be *seen*. So he treated all contacts the same, from the lowest Hadley visitor to the IBM corporation in New York—and got results positively, helping boost Hadley's budget yearly."

A medieval monk once wrote of the blind, ". . . in many perilous situations where men might doubt or dread to go, the blind man, because he sees no danger, is a sure guide."

A bit of prophecy in that!

Richard Kinney, age 11 months

*Dick and his mother on the day of his first trip
to Waring School in Cleveland*

The Kinney family—Hobart, Hope, Dick, and Rosemary

Ron Smith manuals lectures to Dick at Mount Union College

Evelyn and Dick

Dick and Clark

The poet at his Braille typewriter

*Dick, with Jeannie Ridenour, explains Tellatouch
to Prime Minister Gandhi*

Receiving the Anne Sullivan Macy Award from Dr. Peter Salmon;
Jeannie Ridenour in center

"You see . . . and I remember"

EVELYN

It was dark in St. Louis, nearly 2:30 in the morning, and the rest of the family was asleep. Moving slowly in her room, Evelyn Davis reached the desk, inserted a sheet of paper in the typewriter, and began to type a note to her sister. Evelyn was nineteen years old, an honors high school graduate, a young woman ready to begin college at Missouri Valley, a school small enough to assist her, large enough to offer the necessary range of French and Spanish courses for her major. Her family—mother, father, two sisters, and brother—had always encouraged her, made her a part of all their activities; she had done the dishes, cleaned the furniture, taken her place along with them.

College would be different. For a long period she would be away from her friends. Dot, of course, was ready to go along tomorrow, help her with the first days of orientation, help her get acquainted with her new roommate, Elizabeth. Dot could always be counted on to help.

But now, at 2:30, Evelyn had reached a decision after a sleepless night. She started to type:

The reason I'm writing is because I probably won't be awake before you leave. Dottie, I've decided that I won't want you to ask your boss for a day off, and here's why.

Evelyn

My roommate will be there when I arrive. Since I'm going to have to live with Elizabeth for some time, I don't want to start right out by making her feel that there's someone else's opinions and advice that I respect more than hers. She might get the wrong impressions about my wanting her help; and the first impressions you get of a person usually stick the longest . . .

There was another factor in Evelyn's thought that long night. She admitted it in the final lines she typed:

You know, hon, there isn't anyone I'd rather have with me and it's sweet of you to want to go along. But I'm afraid that I'm going to be terribly homesick as it is and if you went along Sunday and had to leave Monday it would just make it that much harder for me.

She had been blind since infancy, eye defects apparent when she was a few months old; the cause was given as cancer of the optic nerve. Her letter that night reflected much of the independence she had to have and the wisdom she acquired—both of which helped her through four years of Missouri Valley College. During those years her sisters were invaluable, recording most of the textbooks for her. Problems, however, developed: since her majors were French and Spanish—and since neither sister knew either language—they had to spell every foreign word on their recordings as they read the texts aloud.

She was graduated with honors in 1955, did additional study at Middlebury and Colby Colleges, then looked for new conquests. She wrote the Sorbonne during her senior year, getting a disappointing, discouraging reply. "We have no special facilities appropriate for the blind," the letter from France said. "Therefore we do not see how we can encourage you to attend." Such judgment was final:

"We would not approve your application because of your circumstances."

What to do about these French officials who refuse to allow her to submit an application because of blindness? Well, she would go ahead on her own, just show up on their doorstep. She'd *show* them she was self-sufficient. On board ship she wrote, "I can hardly wait to get inside that Braille library in Paris. When I get settled I'm going to make several trips to the Sorbonne . . . I'm going to see how many of their texts are available to me in Braille and find out about getting someone to do some reading for me. Then I'm going to wait and tell them I'm there and getting along well. I'll ask them to please reconsider my application."

Then, with perfect logic, she added, "I don't see any argument they can possibly give me then."

She had a great friend and financial supporter in George R. Lantz, owner of a baking company in St. Louis. Inspired by her courage and spirit, he had been responsible for much of her schooling and had agreed to help with expenses for her overseas study as well.

She did her research and several weeks later walked up to the administrative office of the Sorbonne in Paris to introduce herself.

"You have a letter from me," she told them.

They went to their files, found verification of her inquiry and their refusal to admit her. They reread the letters; refusal because she was blind, would require special assistance both in books and personal affairs, assistance they were not prepared to provide.

"Your appearance here today—you came over on ship, found your way here without difficulty?"

Evelyn nodded.

"This has somewhat altered our position."

Now she smiled.

If this young American girl could travel alone, if she could present herself to them without their guidance, well, certainly, they stammered, she could probably be counted on to take care of her classwork as independently. They admitted her.

And later, in her full year overseas, so did the University of Seville in Spain for some special work.

A bird she was, climbing branches one at a time—perhaps several in each leap.

Her schooling went well. She loved the opportunity to talk with others in French, she had good friends along the way, met fellow students from the States who took extra interest in her. Some of the girls established special codes for her; for example, seated at an outdoor cafe, Evelyn and a friend had a young man come up and introduce himself, begin casual conversation. Evelyn's girlfriend shortly afterwards said to her, "Your lipstick is on straight."

Translation: "This guy is cute. And he's not a masher; he's a good type."

Voice helps, but insight of a friend—or is it outreach? —was more helpful.

Perspective. Consider this beginning of a letter from Evelyn to her sisters, recalling a plane trip to Madrid in July, 1956: "There was an elderly French man sitting beside me on the plane . . . he was very nice, but he was almost *too* nice, if you see what I mean."

Well, do we see?

A masher, man on the make?

Evelyn continued, "He cut my meat—which was wonderful—but then he insisted on actually sticking the food in my mouth. I told him to go ahead and eat his own meal, and he insisted that I shouldn't worry about *him*. I didn't know what else to do, so I just let him put olives and strawberries and meat in my mouth. I just wouldn't hurt his feelings."

But hers? "He thought he was really accomplishing something that couldn't be done otherwise."

So, he was too nice. Too nice—and ignorant—to realize that Evelyn had come all the way to Europe without such assistance, was keeping up on her studies, sightseeing, and doing her own eating, thank you, without his smothering help. What she had written was of Evelyn and also of all the others who had long before found independent living.

Again, it was that awareness of her complete self, regardless of the material circumstances, which prompted a smile and trace of a snicker on her face one autumn day in France. With others in her class at the Sorbonne, she was visiting the Pantheon. "And here, ladies and gentlemen," said the guide who, according to Evelyn, apparently knew his speech by heart, "here are the remains of Louis Braille who invented that miraculous method of writing for those poor, unfortunate blind people."

Evelyn smiled broadly.

"Mademoiselle," the guide said sharply, "this is no laughing matter!"

Daily inconveniences were not really problems for Evelyn Davis. Real problems are not the bumps into telephone poles, the hesitant steps off a curb, the unthinking clerks. She found out what real problems could be when she returned from her year of study overseas, deeply impressed with the beauty of the languages, eager to share her awarenesses with young people. Fully certified, fully knowledgeable, she determined next to teach her skills to others. It was then she found out what a "handicapped" person is.

Her applications for teaching jobs were acknowledged, but, not for lack of openings or finances, administrators were turning down Evelyn Davis. They were duly impressed with her grades, her speaking ability, her graduate record, but as soon as she arrived for an interview they began to hold back.

"You're more than qualified," one said, "but young people will take too much advantage of you."

"Someone else will give you the job, but not us."

One administrator said, "If I were a real man and had guts, I'd hire you right now."

Another administrator, during the interview, cried.

But none hired her. A year went by while she kept trying, applying, interviewing. Then, the next summer, while taking a course in Russian at St. Louis University, she met a former teacher of hers, also in the class, who was appalled when she found out why Evelyn was not yet teaching.

"I know one man who will let you try," she said.

That man was Father Curtain of the Catholic school system in St. Louis. At the interview he asked her what her choice of buildings would be. "The biggest coed school in town," was her confident reply.

And, so, among the two thousand young people in the high school she became in 1957 the first blind person to teach in a "normal" coed high school in Missouri—Bishop DuBourg High School. She was to remain on the staff, a highly successful teacher, for five years.

She found companionship wherever she was. Sister Mary Verona, Principal at DuBourg, said that Evelyn's "complete lack of self-pity" had a wholesome effect on the students who were "blessed with so many advantages."

For Evelyn marriage was cherished, and she sought fulfillment with a frail but strong-willed twenty-nine-year-old man, Ray Warmbrodt. Personable, he was doing well in his radio instruction field, but a diabetic condition was robbing him of his sight, restricting his work. Ray and Evelyn met socially, found common ground in their personalities, more than in their handicaps. Their marriage in 1958 was rewarding. They were happy, began buying their own home. Hopes were dashed when Ray's health failed, his body succumbing after long, difficult months to kidney failure.

Should she be fatalistic? Realistic? Idealistic? Her husband was gone, she was alone, a kind of aloneness that differed from the mere independence of her travels, her assertions of individuality and dominion. She returned to education, continued teaching, but sought additional studies so that she could advance. There was a rumor that teachers at Bishop DuBourg school would be called on to do extra work, probably the teaching of American literature in her case. There was a school near Chicago that offered American literature by correspondence—in Braille. The school's promotional folders appealed to her; yes, she'd take a course.

The instructor in American Literature was a man named Richard Kinney.

That name meant nothing to her, of course, but the materials were extremely important. The Hadley School would send along background reading materials of nineteenth century American writers, bulky Braille volumes from the basement library at 700 Elm Street. After receipt, however, she was told all French teachers would continue with their one subject. The first of the volumes went back to Hadley. Dick, receiving them, wrote to urge Evelyn to study the literature for its cultural value. Perhaps there was something of the public relations angle as well, for the letter was very warm and friendly. Dick knew the importance of her position as a blind teacher in a sighted school (she had mentioned this in her correspondence) and was anxious not to lose a "prize student."

A few years later, lining up a trip to the American Association of Workers for the Blind in St. Louis, he remembered Evelyn. "Good chance to get acquainted," he suggested to Cathy Jackson. He wrote Evelyn, saying that if she cared to, she and her teacher could meet and talk things over at the hotel.

This was no special concession; he had arranged to meet students on many trips, so nothing particularly significant was noted about this one; and yet there was the intellectual level of her correspondence, his teaching opportunity, her personality in correspondence as well.

Dick, Cathy, and Hadley's recording engineer, Charles Shipley, boarded the train July 11, 1961, for St. Louis. Prior to the opening meeting that night, they walked down the hotel corridor to the elevator, glided downstairs. Dick could feel the floor dropping under his feet, commented on the ride. Then the motion stopped. Cathy prodded lightly, and they stepped into the lobby. Standing there, a tall, slender, dark-haired woman was smiling. Cathy knew her by the eyes; she wore no dark glasses, but the eyes revealed. Just a year before, Cathy would never have been so alert, but now she made judgments.

In addition, the woman was *waiting*. She acknowledged anticipation in her posture. It was more than eyes.

"Evelyn, so good to see you!" Cathy nodded also to Evelyn's sister, Lois.

"Hi! You must be the Cathy Dick has mentioned."

He stood there, in a dark and unrevealing world. Cathy had stopped walking; something was taking place. Hotel personnel? Directions? Someone from the meeting?

Then the fingers of Cathy into his palm, quick, abbreviated words and his turn to smile. "Hello, Ev!" He extended his hand, Evelyn reached out, guided ever so lightly by Cathy's arm. Then Evelyn put her own fingers in his palm, began to manual her own "hello." She had practiced for this, wanting to impress her teacher. From Hadley literature she had known of the twin impairment.

"The hand certainly adds a personal quality to communication," Dick speaks with authority on this point. "And it certainly added a personal one that time!"

But you didn't fall in love with every girl whose fingers touched your hand!

"No; I guess I had been waiting for lightning to strike. Waiting for more than a decade. Let's just say that the touch made me instantly aware that I was talking to a girl. If it's a slender hand manualing, it adds perceptual transformation to the intellectual intuition, right?"

Later that evening, around the dinner table, Dick asked Cathy, in a tone as guarded as he knew how to control, "She is pretty, isn't she?"

The silent answer then. "Definitely!" Cathy described her hair, her smile. She found herself manualing descriptions "automatically," not really knowing at that moment the deepening awareness growing within Dick's thought about this student.

Recordings of exact conversations sometimes sound silly, for we frequently utilize the simple as key topics. On this occasion, it was a glass of iced tea that became the key; Evelyn spilled her glass—reaching out with her hand and forgetting momentarily where the glass had been. The tea tumbled to the floor in what could have become an awkward, difficult circumstance. She laughed, though, made no attempt to let Dick remain ignorant of the incident, manualed in detail what had happened. Cathy hurried to retrieve the glass and everyone joined in the laughter. Evelyn's manner impressed Dick; she was confident, unassuming, undaunted, spirited. The conversation returned many times to the iced tea and at the end Evelyn let happy fingers romp through Dick's palm to say, "If I get the chance to dine with you again, I promise I won't spill the iced tea!"

The appearance of the dinner group, so involved in fingertip conversation and occasional use of the Tellatouch, caused near chaos in the dining room. People stared, came over for explanations. Cathy, tired of continual interruptions, patiently, quietly, told inquirers.

As Dick talked aloud and Evelyn manualed efficiently, Lois, Cathy, and Charles Shipley decided they were not really needed that evening—not for a while, at least, as the conversation became more and more direct between Dick and Evelyn. They decided to excuse themselves on some pretext of checking out a detail about the meeting rooms for the next day; Dick would be speaking at one of the sessions. An hour later they returned to the dining room to see Dick and Evelyn engaged in continuing conversation. When Cathy touched him to signal her return, he greeted her pleasantly, but added that they were getting along "splendidly." For the first time in his life Dick Kinney may have seen a rainbow in his mind's eye that was not a mere recollection of boyhood days, not a vestige of hues over the outbuildings across the street in little East Sparta after a summer rain, but a rainbow heralding a future rather than a past.

Evelyn returned the next afternoon for luncheon. Now it was Dick who brought up the table talk; he had decided to purchase a small, decorative giraffe he had "seen" on a previous trip. "It felt so beautiful," he told Evelyn. A simple yet delightful ebony carving from Tanganyika. He just had to go to the hotel gift shop to buy it. More important than the Hadley library books, knickknacks and household decorations dominated their conversation.

Later there was a reception line in the hotel in conjunction with the meetings. Evelyn was standing next to Dick when "Cathy had to go on some sort of an errand or something" and manualed the fact that Dick should hold on to Evelyn's hand to keep in line. Apparently someone was shaking both of Evelyn's hands shortly thereafter; in any event, she couldn't hold on to Dick's hand, and someone placed Dick's hand on Evelyn's waist so that he could keep his place in the line.

Now, right in public, Dick had an opportunity to become aware of the fact that, as he says, "I was next to a slender girl with a slim waist . . . this made me aware she was very feminine, shall we say!" Thinking back to this time, he adds, "I was immune to her beautiful brown hair, her smile, and all that, but the sense of touch is powerful!"

Dick has said that he can get a "psychograph" of a person readily. What they say or don't say suggests personality, their shake of hand gives height, their manual a clue to disposition. At the dinner table he had found her hand "warm, dry," her manual "not spasmodic or jerky, not limp either, but at ease and relaxed."

He extended an invitation for this new Hadley student to feel free to visit the school's headquarters sometime in the future. It was a commonplace gesture, but one which obviously carried "a bit more force and meaning" now. If there is such a thing as a twinkle in Dick Kinney's eye, it came when he used this phrasing. For Dick, back in his apartment rooms in Winnetka, above the little English-style town, felt a new loneliness, a longing for a comfortable room filled with laughing, talking people. The check mark on the forehead or shoulder had been important, a tap on the knee as well, but now in his mind there was the touch of a girl who had much skill with the manual and who had fingers that knew much more than others. This girl of "slim waist" and "very feminine touch."

But she lived so far away! She was in St. Louis while he was in that little suburb by Lake Michigan in a third-floor apartment with a view through leafed trees of the Hadley building and Elm and Chestnut—though these were things of his mind, not his sight—and it was not these things but the touch of her hand in a hotel lobby that meant the most. He had extended the invitation for her to visit the school—"partly courtesy, partly hope!"

Evelyn did come to Winnetka to see the school. Treatment accorded her was not exactly that which a "typical" student might have received. Cathy drove Dick to O'Hare to meet her; the teacher does not always make such arrangements, but he wanted very much to greet her personally. They walked to the car, teacher and student, then sat in the rear seat as Cathy drove eastward. Evelyn wore a short-sleeved dress which Dick recalls as "flimsy."

And how did you know that?

"Accidentally touched the dress when I put my palm up for her to manual."

The day was typical of the July heat for Chicago—clear and bright as well. Both of them were aware of such aspects of the day, yet even then they surely sensed implications beyond the typical. For Dick, in recollection, "it was an idyllic romance day" with life abundant, nature kind and generous, and, after all, a flimsy dress equally charitable.

Lunch, then a tour of the school including Dick's office, oversized desk, the split-level library with heavy, bulging steel shelving Braille equipment, the little staff kitchen; they met Peggy Butow at the reception desk, talked with Don Hathaway, other staff members. When the question of the evening meal came up, it was Evelyn's turn. The likely prospect was some kind of grand affair with several staff people joining. She asked Dick, "Do we have to entertain everybody tonight?"

Well, probably not.

"Couldn't we just have something simple together?"

He was delighted. "How about something at my apartment?"

One becomes whatever he must be. Dick had done much cooking for himself, using an electric roaster and a hot plate to advantage. They would find something special for the evening: special even if simple. Cathy went along to get them there safely, then discreetly left till later on. Dick whipped up something "right out of the cans" and topped it off with lemonade.

The courtship, which began in the hotel lobby in a very real sense, was becoming better defined. What better, more appropriate way to conclude the meal than an invitation to chat on the sofa? Evelyn talked about people she had met, and outside the birds had settled on quiet limbs for the night, and below people entered the Sweet Shop for 9 P.M. sundaes and sodas, and the lights at the Hadley parking lot came on, and the Chicago and Northwestern left its final passengers, and time moved in wisps of words and moments for the two of them.

Dick leaned to his left, moving his body consciously even if not fully sure. Evelyn felt his slight touch and she moved as well—towards him.

"I don't know for sure what happened in the next five or ten seconds, but when I came to," Dick says, "I was in love!"

Later, when words returned to both of them, it was Evelyn who interjected the commonplace into their lives again. She would like to have more of that good lemonade that he had made—and she promised not to spill it.

"Unconsciously, we drank then to our future."

The next day they were back at the Hadley building. The basement level contains, among other things, a significant recording studio. Surrounded by glass, it houses equipment for recording tapes and discs for the blind, the work done by volunteers, supervised by Charles Shipley. They came down to the studios that morning; Shipley, remembering the St. Louis meeting, was anxious to point out the variety of equipment being used. After some descriptions, Dick chimed in with a statement that there was a piano. Evelyn suggested they "try it out."

Shipley then discovered that she could play very well. "I could see that the piano was just another bond between them."

Emphasizing chords, Evelyn could produce vibrations for Dick to sense with his hands, even as George Shearing had done—except that that had been in public. Dick suggested "chop sticks" and sat down to play the upper half of the keyboard. They played, talked, Evelyn's fingers moving freely from keys to his palm and back to the keys again.

"Well, I could see it would be a while before they left," Shipley says. Something more important than a mere tour was going on.

Dick Kinney, now thirty-seven years old, found himself thinking about the greatest adventure in his life. Courtship was in order. He could keep in touch with Evelyn after she returned to St. Louis and her own teaching tasks.

Braille letters followed, but within weeks it was evident that the bond between them was more than their academic correspondence. From his bachelor apartment Dick would contemplate a better way—he'd put the telephone to use.

The phone? A long-distance phone? From a fellow who couldn't hear a word, a sound of any kind?

You learn to compensate. Years before, you dropped a dime in the fraternity phone for a cab to go to Polinori's to feel the music of the jukebox—and before that you played ball against the house as a ten-year-old with hearing still there, listening for the return. Now you find yourself in your apartment approaching the phone. You have Evelyn's number and you devise a means of conversation —one-way, but still conversation—with this young lady whose touch has so impressed you.

You pick up the receiver and dial "O."

You wait ten seconds and then say, "Operator, this is Mr. Kinney at Winnetka number 446-1750. I want you to dial a St. Louis number and get Evelyn Warmbrodt on the line. I do not want to speak to anyone else. I am going to hang up now and will wait for ten minutes. As soon as you get her on the telephone please call me at this number. Do not call unless she is actually on the line. If you are unsuccessful within ten minutes please cancel the call."

Then you hang up and place your finger on the phone, as close to the bell under the cover as possible. You will be able to sense the very slight vibration of the bell should your number be called. You are prepared to stand and wait there for ten minutes.

Soon the vibration is sensed. Dick tells it this way: "I'd pick up the receiver, give her the news of the day, and then launch into a dramatic monologue. At times, quite a *romantic* monologue! Trusting, of course, that it was Evelyn and not her brother on the line!"

When he finished his commentary, he placed the receiver down. Evelyn, on the other hand, was keeping track, via notes as well as memory, responding without sounds. Then she would go to her Braille typewriter and respond with the written word to everything he had said —adding questions and comments.

Then her mother would be summoned to take the letter to the main post office immediately—regardless of the time, day or night. Dick had to have her response first thing in the morning.

The method proved highly workable. So much so, that for the next six weeks it increased, almost nightly calls were made by the end of that period. The touch that brought the two of them together had been successfully transferred to the vibration of the telephone bell.

Evelyn once noted that Dick frequently reminded her, "I'm the only man that can get in not only the last word but the *only* word when I call my girl friend!" In any event, it was probably the first courtship in history in which the man did *all* the talking.

One suspects that the nightly romantic monologue was not always a private one. Dick of course, had no way of knowing—until he could get Evelyn's next letter; she might mention extra sounds on the line that she had noticed. And of course there were a few times when the letters would not speak at all of matters Dick had raised in his monologue.

He knew then that he had talked to the wrong person!

Others may have listened in. "Funny thing," he tells, "when we'd break off and say good-bye, I'd feel the click of the receiver—not one, but several, one after the other. I think about six operators were enjoying some of our calls!"

That was just another hurdle for him. And only the listeners know for sure how much of an audience there was. The achievement of conversation with Evelyn was all that really mattered to him anyway. In a speech before the Illinois Bell Telephone Company, Dick later said, after discussing some of the electronic aids for the deaf-blind, that one of their long distance operators was "the second most important woman in my life!"

Regardless of the operator's assistance and curiosity, there was one trick that was strictly private in conjunction with the calls. If he would end the "romantic monologue" with a question, Evelyn would answer after he had hung up by dialing his number and letting it ring only once for yes or twice for no. And if she were so motivated, she would let it ring three times—for "I love you."

Dick's finger stayed close to the bell.

Fascinating, isn't it, that the romance blossomed under such trying circumstances! Remembering how many love affairs come to disaster because of an unwise word, a misread line, a touch or glance in error—with these in mind, the correspondence between these two people is all the more remarkable for its harmony.

During the ten-minute wait till Evelyn came on the line—did you ever get a call from someone *else* during this period and, as a result, give your monologue to the wrong person?

"It happened. Once, maybe twice. But that was just one of the chances I had to take."

All of Evelyn's letters were in Braille, of course; bulky, and perhaps for that reason a bit slower in delivery. The telephone calls were the best source of "conversation" but were quite expensive. Dick laughs: "I finally had to marry Evelyn to keep from going broke on my phone calls!"

From the first Evelyn had been impressed with Dick's strength; she did not like "wishy-washy" people, as Lois phrased it, and found much depth of persistent character in this man. Lois, too, was impressed, and conveyed her reactions to Evelyn as they talked about the meeting in St. Louis, as they talked about the future as well. To her mother, however, Evelyn said little. Lois sensed a guilt complex in this, for despite the relatively recent death of Ray Warmbrodt, here was a man who impressed her in new ways, first with his letters, then with their meetings, then with his distinctive phone conversations. To feel deeply for another was a concern. She had loved Ray very much, but now, life in shambles as a result of the denial to her of a family, of a "normal" life, she wondered deeply if God was opening new channels for her.

Mrs. Davis had to face up to the further obstacles Evelyn was finding in her search for happiness. Lois as well had said little to Mrs. Davis about Dick, except the complimentary remarks. Phone calls were one thing, but the time was approaching when Dick would be visiting the home. "I tried to prepare mother," says Lois, "but I am sure you must realize that until you know someone your eyes carry you away." What Mrs. Davis saw was a rather short man, hesitant in walk after the flight, moving slowly, unseeing, unhearing. "If this is the man you want," she told her daughter, "I only hope with God's strength you will be able to manage. That is all I can hope for."

During the visit to the home Dick cautiously used "Jeff the Giraffe"—the ebony carving he had purchased at the hotel when they first met—as an ego protector, describing him to Evelyn as one with his feet on the ground, his head in the clouds. To this Evelyn said, "Tell Jeff not to be afraid to dream."

She was saying more than words alone. She waited, withdrew her fingers briefly from his palm.

It was time. Dick commented how Jeff would enjoy feminine companionship. "You know, he'd like a cooling hand to dry his fevered brow." Other indirections followed.

Evelyn's fingers flew back into his palm, still opened,

resting in his lap; fingers moved rapidly, interrupting his comment. "Never mind that darned giraffe," the fingers protested. "Speak for yourself, Dick!"

He proposed. She accepted.

They were engaged six weeks after the long-distance phone calls had begun, but the marriage would not take place for almost another nine months. She would finish her teaching contract. In addition, they felt that time was a helpful ally. "Love at first sight means an intuitive attachment, a sympathy between people," Dick said. "But it should be confirmed by physical, mental, spiritual day-to-day contact against the friction of living."

When visiting Hadley again, Evelyn tried more tunes on the piano, different rhythms. Dick suggested some from his boyhood, even started singing a bit. The problem, of course, despite the unevenness of his voice, was not the voice nor the melody nor the delight of the two at the piano. It was the irony of the site—the studio was the most public room in the entire building—and the hallways running past the huge glass windows surrounding the room were used by the staff. Charles Shipley recalls: "You felt like a peeping Tom. Here they were in love and here we were watching every move. I had work to do in the control room adjacent, but I couldn't concentrate—and didn't think I should even be around."

The staff took measures to help. Shipley pulled curtains over the windows, phased out his electronic equipment, simply closed the studio as much as he could. He went upstairs and pretended he was busy reading mail and repairing equipment and getting a drink and talking to others and everyone understood; before long anyone who did walk down the studio corridor was reminded of his offense by the curtained walls. A sign above the studio door read "Quiet" and inside the quiet fingertip words, the closeness of the two persons on the piano bench, the soft melodies, all became part of the quiet love in Dick Kinney's life.

During the spring Evelyn flew to Akron to be met there by the Kinney family and driven to East Sparta for a visit of several days.

"She's very intelligent," Dick had assured his parents. They found that out, but only after a brief encounter with shyness—a shyness not in keeping with the rest of Evelyn's character, but perhaps one appropriate for a prospective bride. Dick had already been home for the visit, drove to the airport with his family, had them primed for the reception. At home they played cribbage, some cards, talked about the village. They didn't go far from the house. Hobart Kinney told them he was tiring of the hardware business now; a year later he sold out. They walked to the building one evening.

Hope Kinney was thrilled with the turn of events in her son's life; she knew he was finding his own avenues of achievement, that marriage to this lovely blind girl would complement everything else he had done. What if she had not felt that way? "We didn't argue with Dick's decisions; he'd been right so many times!"

The First Congregational Church in Winnetka is a picturesque red brick structure, white steepled above its sanctuary from the sides of which offices stem. To get to them you follow sidewalks paralleling a porch, and you think you are nearing some pleasant ranch-style house. Beyond the offices and overhang is the chapel, an extra structure but no afterthought, its steps winding effectively to Pine Street which wraps itself around the church block.

The marriage ceremony was in the chapel on this happy day, an exultant little chapel with lofted podium, with alternate marbleized dark green and white floor tiles like some chess board, and seating in six pews for more than one hundred persons.

Did they have concerns about the marriage? They knew the happiness, the fruition, the rightness, and the dominion already expressed would only be expanded in this union. The couple had their own sentiment: "We knew we could solve any problems together. If either one of us had started worrying about what might go wrong, we'd never have had the enthusiasm to believe in what would be right with us."

It was a very special June day, its impact going beyond the bounds of the chapel. Harry Semrow, acting postmaster of the giant Chicago post office, who knew of Dick through the Hadley school mail volume, wrote, "Thirty thousand people in the Chicago post office are celebrating the fact that you are going to get married. We are all happy for you and your bride, and I think I am going to tell all of the mailmen of Chicago to put a little note in everybody's mailbox saying how lucky Dick Kinney is." He added, "Maybe we should say how lucky the girl is to get a grand guy like you!"

At the 4 P.M. ceremony Marshall Berman was the best man, helping to manual the rites. One thing for sure: there were many hands actively involved in the ceremony! Evelyn, of course, manualed as the wedding kiss moment arrived. She had said to others prior to the ceremony that she thought she'd manual the "basics" of the admonitions of the Rev. Ernest Yarrow—"You know, the parts about 'honor' and 'obey' but maybe not the rest!"

With all the manualing going on, the Rev. Yarrow at one point talked about "joining all four hands" when calling for placing of the rings; it was a double ring ceremony. Despite this temporary lapse (which prompted chuckles throughout the chapel) the rings were exchanged satis-factorily.

Evelyn's brother, Allen, gave her away; matron of honor was Dick's sister, Rosemary. Rounding out the wedding party was Cathy Jackson as bridesmaid. Don Hathaway was proud to be an usher, as was Rosemary's husband, Dr. Willard H. Hartup. Evelyn's sisters, Lois and Dottie, their families, Mrs. Davis, Hope and Hobart Kinney, many of the Hadley staff, and a host of friends filled the chapel.

A reception followed, the couple then anxious to leave. Many offered their services to speed them to the airport where a room was reserved at the Sheraton Motel prior to the early morning flight to the west coast. They could have taken any of a dozen different cars, but were adamant in turning down the offers. "We'll go ourselves. Just us."

And so around 8 P.M. they crawled into a taxi; Evelyn told the driver the Sheraton at O'Hare, and with a final wave to their friends they sped off to the pleasant motel room with private terrace.

"I don't recall that we ever got to the terrace," says Dick.

Earlier that evening, during the reception, someone came up to Evelyn saying there had been a long distance phone message for her husband. No need for him to go to the phone, of course; the message had already been given. It was shared with Evelyn who, in turn, manualed it to Dick.

The message was from Ron Smith of Mount Union College days; he just wanted to remind Dick that Evelyn certainly was no department store mannikin!

TOGETHER

Near the La Hacienda Motel, honeymoon quarters in San Francisco, the touch of wind upon your face brings hints of moisture. Cool, intermittent sun, with wind picking up. Then in the car driven by Merry Leary, formerly your secretary back in Winnetka—she and her husband are now hosting this sightseeing trek. Then walking the wide rim of the Golden Gate bridge while cars are intent on Sausilito or up the coast. You sense them. But, better, the bridge begins talking to you under your feet. The wind speaks in many languages, and cars add throbs. "There must be many cars."

Merry confirms. Then more dampness and then the singing of the wind.

"I love sightseeing!"

Now, how can that be? You, who see nothing, never hear the slightest sound. What is there to sightseeing?

"Have you ever seen the Golden Gate bridge?"

Of course.

"Did you get out of the car? You probably drove right across it, seeing blue waters and the sun glint on arched girders."

For Dick? "I put my hands on the steel cables, I felt

the vibrations through them! It was a very *personal* encounter. I found the touch of her language, and under my feet she danced in the wind. Exhilarating!"

Yet the touches were not always enough beyond the bridge. For both of them there was the Sherlock Holmes element in their honeymoon; each day, each moment was a type of puzzle, pieces to be put together, fragments of a picture only. From clues of touch and motion the world is defined.

But how to interpret a clue?

The honeymoon was not without a terror. On their first night in the motel the sliding door to the patio opened and then closed—the work perhaps of a prankster. Although Dick locked the door after being told of the circumstance of opening by Evelyn, she remained apprehensive. As the evening went on she became more and more concerned that there was, indeed, an intruder in their quarters. Here, her depth perception was of little use; fears mounted that there was someone or something hiding in the bathroom ready to rob or pillage later in the evening.

Dick knew of all the big city stories of thievery, murder. This was no simple matter, but what could one deaf-blind person do? To ascertain in the first place whether someone was there—steps, sounds, movements beyond his touch were unknown. And how could he take any protective measures anyway? He could hardly try a fist fight or a fast draw! There was a phone, of course, but the intruder could hear their message and attack quickly if they should have to speak into the phone. Evelyn, transmitting her fears to Dick by fingertips, had made no sound whatever.

Bride and groom were unable to perceive the nature of the danger. Terror of this kind had never struck their lives before, but perhaps Evelyn was thinking back several years to a time when she was a student in France, alone in her boardinghouse room, with windows barred—and yet this strange movement on her bed. A sound, a motion setting thoughts running in tangents. That night, as a frightened blind student, she had ducked under covers and pictured a rat or two at bed's end.

Then, mustering desperate nerve, she had bolted from the bed, into a hallway, screaming. Friends came—and discovered a cat nestled in folds of her blanket. A cat who had given birth to kittens on another bed another time and had the same in mind that night, had Evelyn not made her fear known.

Out of darkness, phantasms came in this honeymoon time. She had no other answers, and with the same kind of desperation she and Dick talked about it, Evelyn manualing her fears into his responsive hand.

Realizing the full measure of terror which had come to her, Dick drew himself up and decided to take bold action. He removed a heavy shoe and approached the bathroom, shoe raised in defiance of whatever evil lurked there. "Feeling a bit like Dagwood Bumstead," he recalls, "I crept to the shower feeling my way along the paneling." Was someone there, hiding behind the shower curtain?

Did that person know of the raised shoe? Would an arm come out, send Dick reeling, send an unknown wall into his head?

Trembling, Dick flung back the curtain. "I delivered a mighty blow, slashing down across the area and crashing right into the faucet!"

In retrospect, after the realization came fully that no one was intruding in any way, they could laugh about it. And Dick later said, "There I was, ready to defend my little bride against a mighty intruder!" He added carefully, "I think I was a little proud of myself, too, for trying it."

Had somebody played a joke on them? Even if so, Dick had his last laugh. His stature rose even more in Evelyn's thought, if that were possible. Bumstead had risen to the occasion with a victory, and she was impressed with it.

The days at San Francisco ended, and the honeymooners said their good-byes to their friends. Aloft again, they were returning after a stop in Denver.

The apartment was ready for them after the honeymoon. Now home, they came into the entrance way, turned right to the simple living room, a sofa, card table serving as his desk, several chairs; from there they could see—well, visitors could see—the wrought iron dinette set in the alcove, kitchen beyond. To the left of the entrance was the bedroom and bath. Evelyn had no plans to alter the furnishings; they were pleasant for their needs. She enjoyed opportunities to get acquainted with neighbors—the Geisers, in particular, whose grandchildren she loved to hold and talk to.

In evenings Dick had enjoyed visiting the Sweet Shop, with its soda fountain and friendly environment. Previously he had to rely on Hadley friends who would stop by the apartment to escort him. The Jordans, the Bermans were specially close. Now, with Evelyn at his side, they could go whenever they wished; she, too, enjoyed the little corner restaurant and its atmosphere. Dick Tsitsis, manager, in turn always had a special welcome out for them. Other stores were close by, and Evelyn loved to shop throughout the business area. She assumed all grocery chores, concentrating, admittedly, on frozen foods and TV dinners more than most customers did.

It was an idyllic summer for the two of them. Winnetka

is almost a fantasy suburb, its range of economic back-grounds not so diverse as to produce ghettos, but it does include elitisms. Dick Kinney did not roam the privately-patrolled sections, but he had always been known by those who did. He was special. Now, Evelyn was received as well, proudly, in fact, by storekeepers, circle of volunteer workers for the Hadley School, townspeople.

Another marriage took place in 1962; Cathy Jackson then decided to spend full time in her new home, thus bringing about another job interview, another need for Dick to select a secretary. That summer this ad appeared in the papers:

Attractive opening for intelligent, personable young woman under thirty as secretary to Richard Kinney, deaf-blind Assistant Director of the Hadley School. Good typist, able to drive car, free for several short business trips annually to various parts of the country. Challenging work, interesting people. Chance to meet the public. Hillcrest 6-8111.

Mrs. Jeannie Ridenour was among those who read the ad with interest. Wife of a public school teacher in nearby Northfield, she was then working in the public relations office of United Airlines. "Few short trips" seemed appropriate, "deaf-blind" aroused curiosity. Now, just what would all that involve? Her husband encouraged her to check it out. Three days later she interviewed, one of many who answered the ad. She didn't have much of an idea, perhaps was only mildly interested, but she found herself—as so many others had—drawn magnetically to this fascinating personality whose life depended so much on fingertips. He was gregarious, affable, incisive in his questions, and yet put her at ease. Jeannie found herself *wanting* the job, wanting to know more about the deaf-blind. Her public relations work helped her cause, and on that basis, plus his judgment of her personality and adeptness, Dick selected her, terminating other interviews. It proved to be the best of all selections, beginning a relationship second only in meaning to Dick and Evelyn's. Yes, 1962 was a vintage year for people in Dick Kinney's life.

His travels in conjunction with fund raising for the school and its overall public relations continued to expand. Early that fall Dick found himself flying to New York City with his wife. Their stay was for three days: meetings of the American Foundation for the Blind occupied first thought, but there was time for some sightseeing as well.

The newlyweds found time to do some shopping by themselves, exploring streets together. Evelyn did not use a cane, despite the unfamiliarity with the streets. Back in Winnetka she had done shopping with many clerks never realizing her blindness. Dick used the cane; she used her ears. The two of them had all the necessary awareness. Evelyn was a daring traveler—and Dick felt he had to display confidence—"usually with fingers crossed!"

Riveters and the noise of the city, of cabs, buses, trains, did not help Evelyn's echo perception, however; she needed to ponder distance of buildings from the feedback of sounds and so occasionally was confused. "We made it though. Bought Evelyn a pair of low-heeled shoes that afternoon. She knew just what she wanted."

Back in Winnetka, in the early autumn of a joyous new time of his life, Dick thought about his poems. It was time to collect the pamphlets he had published a decade before, those little collections sold in conjunction with his lectures, poems intended to help support himself, poem-opportunities that had attracted Don Hathaway among others. *Flutes Beyond the Day,* an early collection, had served its purpose; now another musical reference was in order, something to help celebrate his happiness. Flutes became a harp, and the new collection hardbound this time. He titled it *Harp of Silence,* fifty-three poems together with an introductory statement by Hathaway.

Now it was the time to write the poem of universals, of all and yet peculiarly of himself and his wife. Talking to you and to me, his poem began to unfold that summer rather quickly, its message one of worlds unlimited—certainly a universal—and yet within the poem a genuine, sharp authentic of Evelyn and himself. It was a poem for her, about her, to her. Reading it, however, we can find Dick Kinney within it always, speaking to us . . . and of us, and for us.

> *Through rain and rainbows let us walk*
> *And pause and ponder as we talk*
> *Of beauty, burning like an ember,*
> *That you see . . . and I remember.*
>
> *Let us lean against the sky*
> *Westward where the echoes die,*
> *Each sound that your quick ear gives*
> *Sifted for me through silent sieves . . .*

Together we can move even as the sun towards beauty that lies deep, burning, feeling—and with sounds, the irony of silent sounds. Then the sharpness of love:

> *Once upon a sunshine-dappled day,*
> *I heard a blind girl, musing, say,*
> *"I cannot see the stars, but I*
> *Enfold within my soul a sky!"*

147

Together

> *So if the sky enfolding you*
> *Bends close about us, then we two*
> *Walk with a sky within, without . . .*
> *Heavens about us, all about!*
>
> *And every bird-enchanted breeze*
> *Gathers us treasures from the seas!*
> *And every flower from the life-lush sods*
> *Fountains us nectar from the gods!*
>
> *Dream upon dream, our pulses beat*
> *With dust and stars beneath our feet—*
> *With stars and dust that, overhead,*
> *Beckon to worlds unlimited.*
>
> *Through veils and vistas let us walk*
> *And pause and ponder as we talk*
> *Of beauty that we'll share together,*
> *All in the rain and rainbow weather.*

He dedicated the poem to Evelyn who had, indeed, walked with him through veils, vistas, rain—and what now surely was true—the rainbow time. As the edition was in the final stages, he dedicated the book also to her: "For Evelyn, for whom the harp of silence plays."

In the nineteenth century Emily Dickinson had written

> *The brain is wider than the sky,*
> *For, put them side by side,*
> *The one the other will include*
> *With ease, and you beside.*

For him the enfolding sky was bending close by the two of them, but it was a sky *within;* isn't that what Emily Dickinson was saying in her own way? Her mind could encompass the sky, still have room for more. Dick and Evelyn had the sky within their thought, beyond star glitter, sunset trail, even beyond the sound of rain; within was the symbolic rainbow for both of them.

Evelyn's role in his life gained even more attention. On an October night in 1962 trustees of the Hadley School met in the conference room for their monthly meeting. Assistant Director Kinney joined in all such meetings, this evening accompanied by Evelyn. Discussions of finances, enrollment, equipment, innovations, public relations went routinely. Hathaway gave the bulk of the reports; Dick spoke of fund raising efforts, several promotions within the staff, some new students—and of the population of Winnetka.

As the meeting closed, Jeannie Ridenour manualed to him the final approvals, said "adjournment." Dick then spoke out in a voice wavering perhaps a bit more now than it had earlier in that evening. He wanted to make a statement, he said, regarding enrollment and the general Winnetka community. Trustees stopped folding papers, wondered what addendum this was, turned in their chairs towards him.

Jeannie did not know what he was going to say.

Evelyn did not know he would say it just *then*.

"It is my sure knowledge," he began, measuring his words, "that the population of Winnetka is going to go up by at least one more come next May."

He paused, then started again, but by now Jeannie was manualing frantically as the trustees, grasping the significance of his remark, began to talk at once. Such delight was seldom seen before in the staid meetings. It broke up in glee.

Dick and Evelyn would become parents in the spring.

"Evelyn was a bit upset about my public announcement," he admits, "but I just couldn't resist it. The ham in me, I guess!"

He would never see or hear his child. But he would become a father.

There are many ways to define love. It can be, significantly, a sudden yet constant desire to share oneself by being a part of another's wish. As winter moved and Evelyn's pregnancy became more manifest, Mrs. Geiser, next door, offered her a dress appropriate for her condition. A gift from the neighbors. She was delighted, fondling it with much appreciation.

"What color is it?"

"Blue."

"Oh, wonderful! That's Dick's favorite color!" She ran hands over the material. "Blue is such a beautiful color, isn't it!"

Mrs. Geiser was pleased as well, then asked, "Evelyn, do you know what *blue* is?"

Now a pause, extending itself as a faint smile finally emerged. Softly, she replied, "No."

But that did not really matter. Dick had seen, many years before, what blue was. He would like the dress knowing that it was blue. She would tell him it was blue.

Spring, 1963. Time had passed, the child now near time of birth, the first child of a deaf-blind person with a college education; that which had not been a part of Helen Keller, not a part of the experience of Bob Smithdas, now to be fulfilled for Dick Kinney. There were no abnormalities expected, but Evelyn was told that the birth would have to be encouraged artificially. She could, in fact, select the day for this to be done. According to Jeannie, Evelyn was "much like a Cheshire cat, grinning and enjoying it all so much."

She chose the first day of May for her child's birth. In the morning Jeannie drove to the apartment, as she had done throughout that winter when she would come to the door, chat with the two of them, then escort Dick to the Hadley building just a block away. Now on this first May morning she hurried up the steps, found her friends waiting. Evelyn was not, however, quite ready for the trip to the hospital. She wanted a favor.

"Let's go to the Sweet Shop first. I'd like a hot chocolate."

They sat at a corner table of the little restaurant. Jeannie manualed the conversation; Evelyn was becoming a bit subdued, one of the few times in her life. She had wanted a child for a long, long time: back in her school days she had always spoken of becoming a mother; her delight with the Geiser grandchildren was so happy a part of her life in Winnetka. Love for family was deep, genuine. Perhaps motherhood was part redemption for her, for other denials. She did not speak of these things as she finished the morning hot chocolate, but Jeannie knew her thoughts were deep.

The three went to the hospital; Dick and Jeannie spent most of the day in the room with Evelyn. Consider the circumstance of the father-to-be relying that day as he had throughout most of his life on the sense of touch. No, there was no attempt to deprive him of this day by the attendants. He could stay, place his hands on his wife's body; he must share in this travail.

Through this time Evelyn was not able to manual conveniently, her position and temporarily slower movement of the muscles in her hands working against this. Jeannie listened to her, manualed efficiently to Dick as he reached out with one palm, keeping the other on Evelyn, sharing thoughts and touches throughout the day. Touch—he had said a "slim waist" had brought them together—and touch would not be denied their mutual experience now.

151

Just prior to birth late that afternoon, Evelyn may have had a moment of great fear perhaps, according to Jeannie, the "only one she had ever had to that time." She moved quickly to one side, seemed to stare directly at Jeannie and then said, "Tell him. Tell Dick that I love him. Be sure to tell him." Then she turned away sharply.

Moments later, now in the waiting room, he sat with Jeannie as she manualed those words. They made idle conversation, then waited. On his lap he held the Tellatouch, fingering keys, drumming against the sides. Time of fruition and time of fear. Time of faith. Jeannie's fingers touched occasionally, reassuring. He waited.

Jeannie's finger again, she was moving the Tellatouch; someone would be using it now.

"Oh, good. We have some word, do we?"

He placed his finger on the receiver cell, fingertip to the world. A dot pattern popped into it and he knew Dr. Morley was giving the message; Jeannie would have manualed. Slowly, too slowly, he found letters, pushed in sequence creating the thrust of dots, spelling out the arrival of a baby for the Kinney family.

"Great!"

Then more dot patterns saying, "He's a chip off the old block."

"Then it's a *boy?*"

"Yes."

And Evelyn was doing fine.

No fingertip message had ever been so meaningful for him. His voice, always wavering and with emphasis frequently misplaced, was joyous as he thanked the people at the hospital, repeated again for Jeannie the fact that the baby was a boy. Her fingers gave happy replies, and he felt simple punches and movements in them of great emotion as well. Other persons in the corridor enjoyed the scene.

From the hospital Jeannie made calls to Mrs. Davis, the Kinneys in East Sparta, and to the Hadley School where a celebration would take place that day.

Later, after the exultant news, the chance to touch Evelyn again, and much reporting from Jeannie on the appearance of the baby, he sat alone in the apartment as he had been for eight years before the marriage; at a conventional typewriter he wrote his parents and Mrs. Davis: "What a glorious day! Everyone says he is a beautiful baby, healthy, and honey-haired and bright-eyed. He arrived this afternoon around 2:40 and by now Evelyn has no doubt flashed you word by phone. She was planning to call St. Louis as I tottered away for a couple of hours of rest here at the apartment, before going back to the hospital for an evening visit."

To Mrs. Davis he enclosed a check to cover travel expenses. Evelyn had not made any urgent request that her mother be there, but Mrs. Davis wanted to join in the days of return to the apartment.

Dick closed his letter by saying, "Evelyn is just radiant!"

They had both wanted a boy. The unborn baby had always been referred to as "he" in their conversation both between themselves and with others. Now their dream was fulfilled. Dick Kinney was now the father of a young son. Evelyn found her motherhood.

They named the baby Clark. Allen Clark Kinney.

It was a rainbow day for all three of them.

His eyes were bright, his ears receptive; no sensory perception inadequacy at all.

Once back in the apartment the Kinneys had loving assistance whenever they needed it—long after the grandmothers had concluded their visits. The Geisers were particularly alert, helping Evelyn read the thermometer, helping with the eyedropper, helping with diapers.

Lisa, the Geisers' granddaughter, had been a favorite with Evelyn the previous winter; now some of the tenderness and gaiety she had for the little girl, just a year old, was added to her deep love for her own child. She took extra care with Clark, overcoming every problem with patience and ingenuity. How could she be sure he was eating his food in right amount? When he began to take some strained baby foods, she began to feed him by inserting a tube in his mouth, gently coaxing the food into the tube so that he could not avoid it. There were dangers with this method, of course: she might be too forceful, he might gag; but her tender words and understanding ways minimized the dangers.

She had many moods, cried on occasion, knew frustrations. She could not handle all problems alone. Once, while Clark was learning to crawl around, she dropped a glass on the floor, heard it hit and shatter. She got down with careful moves to pick up the pieces, but how could she ever be sure they were all removed? No concern for her own welfare now, a few jags of glass on her fingers were not the alarm; it was Clark's moves later. In this case she called the Geisers immediately, had them check the entire kitchen floor before she was satisfied.

The Geisers were very accommodating; just as they had kept their eyes on Dick, they embraced Evelyn and Clark in their outreach. One morning they raised a question about lighting; neither of the Kinneys ever turned on lights after dark, of course; fixtures as unnecessary then as at high noon. They mentioned this to Evelyn, who was a bit amused at their inquiry.

"We don't need the light," she said. "You know that."

"But your baby needs it."

Evelyn was stunned. "I never thought of it. Never at all!" She brooded over this, made sure lights were switched on after that. It was another remembering that Dick and Evelyn had to reach out to understand.

But they were used to reaching out.

They caused considerable alarm for some authorities. With Clark five weeks old, a door knock one day announced arrival of a health department representative, a woman who visited all homes of the newly born, checking up on sanitation, health certificates, child care facilities. During the informal interview she became aware of the mother's blindness, finding this incompatible with some predetermined judgments.

"You mean you can't see at all?"

"No."

"Oh, dear me, this isn't right. You can't *see* your baby?"

"No. But I know he is with me."

"Does his father take care *completely* when he comes home? He must have a lot to face up to."

"His father is deaf-blind."

"He's *what?* You mean he—" She was unable to get the words.

"His father loves the baby just as much as I do."

"But, if he can't *hear,* and if—"

"We know where Clark is, we get along very well."

"But this simply is not right. Why, we've never *heard* of this kind of situation before—"

At this point Clark showed his own sentiments by filling his diapers. Evelyn said she'd have to excuse herself.

The next afternoon, feeding the baby, Evelyn heard the door again. "I'm busy!" she explained.

"Dear me, how can you do that?"

The health department was back again. Evelyn refused to come to the door—she was busy with more important matters—and later that day manualed to Dick about the second call; he, in turn, wrote the hospital requesting the health department to back off. He appreciated the concern, but it was not warranted.

Reluctantly, the department scheduled no more visits.

Evelyn, however, had to face up to concerns of her own.

Feeding Clark one morning, having him perched jauntily in his high chair, she noticed that, although he was eating, his head did not seem to be upright—not as he had held it before. She put hands over his face, confirming. She raised the head, encouraging him to keep it up, but he let it drop. She could feel it sagging, now at times almost touching the tray of the chair.

She was alarmed now. Was there some muscular problem? Was it beginning to manifest itself? She tried again, but again the head sagged.

Then a cheery hello from Jeannie Ridenour, stopping by, just to see if Evelyn needed anything. Jeannie sensed the alarm right away.

"I'm concerned, Jeannie. About Clark, I can't figure out why his head is drooping—it's been this way all through the feeding."

Rushing to the chair, Jeannie put her hands to Clark's head, fearful, and then saw him hold his head briefly before drooping once again almost to the tray.

"He did it again, didn't he?"

"Yes." Jeannie searched for some reason. There had to be a reason.

"He's never been this way before—" Evelyn's distress mounted.

No, he hadn't been like that. Fortunately, however, a sighted person could put the pieces of this puzzle together; Jeannie realized moments later what was happening. Clark before had never noticed his own image in the highly polished stainless steel tray—but he caught it now! On this morning he was so fascinated by that image, he wanted to keep inspecting. There was no muscle problem, no loss of proper action. After the explanation the two women had a good chuckle over it.

At nightime the baby slept in his parents' room. Evelyn would never let him be more than a few feet away. She was a person who enjoyed devising her own solutions to the practical dilemmas she faced. Carrying Clark while she went outside, down Elm Street to Lakeside Foods, the Sweet Shop, or any other of the stores was a bit dangerous, but she loved holding him over her shoulder as she made her excursions. Down the block from 723 Elm was the village barber shop which she would pass each morning on such trips. Next door was the Sweet Shop. The barbers were friendly men who enjoyed her personality and reveled in her display of her child; they talked frequently with her as she walked by, but they were deeply concerned about the dangers on these jaunts: young bicyclists frequently propped their bikes against the trees along the sidewalks, occasionally even let the bikes drop to the walk when they would rush in for a haircut. There was no curb lawn for the bikes, so they had to be propped somewhere else.

What if Evelyn tripped over one of the bikes as she walked along some pleasant morning, holding Clark as she did against her shoulder? She would never see the bikes, never be able to protect the child. The barbers were nervous—more nervous, apparently, than she was. When Evelyn kept on with her walks, the men of the barber shop took their concerns to City Hall and got a response which brought a measure of safety.

Response that remains today, when Clark is no longer being held by his mother on morning walks. Today in

Winnetka you see signs along the commercial areas: "No Parking Bicycles in This Block." The police department has decided to let the ordinance remain.

Later, when Clark grew heavier, Evelyn found another way to go about with him, a way disconcerting to her friends for other reasons, but a solution typically Evelyn's. She had an old utility table with casters on it, a table hardly intended to hold passengers—but one she found was just right in height for Clark to be wheeled from room to room. In addition, with it she could wheel Clark to the elevator, then to the sidewalk, to her shopping. No expense involved, just a strap to secure the little fiberglass baby carrier she placed on top of the table. The sight of it disturbed some of her friends—after all, it was so makeshift and seemed so inappropriate—but Dick, never having seen a readymade equivalent of the "Clarkmobile," as she called it, found no fault.

You see, Evelyn had solved her own problem. On her own she had faced up to the possibilities and did what she could do. Dick could appreciate such achievement.

The young family was an ideally happy one. Dick loved to trace Clark's form, cooed to him (as best he knew what that meant), held him, learned to help feed him, enjoyed getting on the carpet and playing with his son, with finger touches and long strokes; Evelyn would manual every reaction that Clark gave which she could understand.

It was a notable year, and May a notable month. Three weeks after the birth of Clark, Dick became the first deaf-blind person to receive the Society of Midland Authors Citation for "Meritorious Service." The banquet in his honor was held May 24; it was then that Henry Rago, distinguished editor of the old and highly respected magazine *Poetry,* spoke warmly of Dick's writing. To the audience Rago said, "Richard Kinney has taught us to see what cannot be seen and to hear what cannot be heard."

In the apartment as Clark continued to grow, the rooms seemed smaller. Clark would need a yard soon, surely by the next springtime he would be ready to roam in a backyard. The apartment had served its purpose well, but something larger was in order.

A little home, bungalow style of the 1920s, became available just west of the town center, about five blocks from Hadley School.

On Elm Street it was—one is tempted to conclude that all addresses in Winnetka are those of Elm Street—at 896. Jeannie Ridenour was asked her opinion as well as Don Hathaway and others. All concurred. Of gray stucco, the house was one of three identical structures perched in a row on 35-foot by 120-foot lots with driveways abutting the walls of the adjacent homes. Five steps to the postage stamp front porch made it a bit difficult for Dick, but the location was ideal, space much more than they had had, and the price was right. They purchased and moved in in February of 1964.

Clark was then ten months old. It was a time of father and son getting more acquainted; they started living room romps and tussles, made rudimentary "Hello's" and "Good-bye's." Dick liked to stretch out on the carpet or the bed; Evelyn would place Clark on Dick's stomach; then tracing the form of his son again, Dick would touch lips, hair, fingers, ears—and wonder about the sounds Clark was making when lips parted. If something was wrong, Evelyn's fast fingers worked into his palm, flashing key syllables.

But most of the time you felt the touch of the little body against your chest, a touch matched only by the glow within yourself with each little movement the child made.

For most of us the sense of touch becomes taboo after the age of eight or nine, but for Dick "it never goes out of style!" And there were in that winter the beginnings of special touches between the two of them that would be incomprehensible to other persons. Touches in special spots just like back on campus—the forehead check, the right knee, thumb and forefinger on shoulder. Now not only identification of person but of emotion as well. Clark learned these touches without schooling, they came naturally over long months and repeated actions. When he learned that crying came from unhappiness, and the crying meant tears from the eyes down his face, he learned as well to trace finger lines down his father's cheek—and his father came to learn that his son was crying.

Certain pokes and punches—lightly given—came to say "I understand," and "I'm having fun." Dick did not hesitate to speak aloud to Clark, words that Evelyn was sure to hear, and Clark in turn spoke up even though it took the touches for words to have meaning. Growing times, happy times for the little family in the bungalow.

Dick had found fruition for himself as he continued to teach and reach out to the nameless numbers of others who had never known this kind of deep personal warmth without seeing or hearing.

BLACK BOUGHS AND MARIGOLDS

July, 1964. The warm sun dances across the white streets of Winnetka, filtered through wide maples. The sun was always something they could both *feel*. Warm, penetrating, it evoked much comment. Like the feel of their child, now just more than a year old. Clark and the day; the sunshine of their lives.

It was not more than they had every right to ask for; there was no penalty about to come because of their prosperity, their mountaintop gained. If one believes in penalties, he finds it difficult to believe in rewards; what they had gained was of dominion, not limitation.

This July was a time, however, of recollection of the past. The baby of the past was now Evelyn; again the eye defect which had caused loss of sight at the youngest age, vestige of malignant, unwanted misfunction in earliest years having taken heavy toll—now in this warm July day it loomed again following a checkup. Their marriage only of two years, and that is such a brief time; and yet within another month Evelyn is forced to spend much of her time in the back room at 896 Elm, on the double bed staring into a nothingness that grows within her mind.

Is this to be the way it must all end?

To stare into voids? Not voids of sight, but, worst of all, voids of the mind?

They would overcome this. There was quiet faith that had been with them in times of knowing; a faith manifest without ritual, more with confidence which must remain. They had known the dregs of continual medical aid, yet found faith in something more than medicine. A visitor once noted several pills that had spilled from a table to the floor. With Clark crawling, this might be a tricky, possibly dangerous situation. To this Evelyn replied, "We'll do all we can and then have faith. Faith in God has brought us this far." The pills were picked up, of course, but there were other days, other times of the unseen fingers of spiritual faith touching their thought just as their own fingers were tracing actions. They had to go on more than what others *saw*.

Now, every specialist was tried, every known treatment, yet it became evident that increasingly Evelyn was deteriorating. From her bed she talked continually to little Clark, then with fingers still nimble, assuring Dick.

By November, 1964, the outlook was very bad. Still, November, as planned earlier that year, was to have been a time of fine new achievement. There had been much encouragement for Dick to give a reading of his poems for the Winnetka area. During his trips he readily used his poems in inspirational talks, found them cropping up in much business conversation and correspondence. It was time to have a lecture on poetry for his own home town. They had decided on November, on Evelyn's birthday.

Harp of Silence, dedicated to Evelyn, had been published two years before. He decided to title the program from the book, read selections, comment on his poetry: a poetry teacher sharing his own creative labors. Community Hall on Lincoln Street was selected, a guest list prepared. Originally, any income from the lecture would have gone to the Hadley school program. Now, however, after some more planning sessions, it was decided by friends that the program go entirely for Evelyn. When you bought a ticket you were giving to the mounting expenses in the search for better health for her.

It would be wonderful to have Evelyn join the others in Community Hall. Mrs. Davis, Mrs. Kinney, friends from school were taking care of Clark more and more, scheduling visits for days and weeks. She would enjoy the words, sense the response so much better than Dick. The poems —from "Invitation" on—were of deep meaning for her. Friends talked about how they might arrange to have her present, but the verdict was negative; she could not leave the bed. Marcia Berman then had an idea: why not use a loudspeaker system in some manner—perhaps through a phone system—and beam the entire program into the home?

Illinois Bell Telephone was glad to cooperate, sending technicians to Community Hall that day without charge, providing the entire system.

That evening, with three hundred persons in the audience, Jeannie assisted Dick on the platform, then joined the others listening as he spoke of life, of poetry, of words that would be "Silent if they must, but music if they can."

The Hall, a rambling gray stone building, was more like an ivy league dormitory—or those at Northwestern University just a few miles south—than a municipal building. A courtyard entrance added charm. The theater where he spoke was at the end of a lobby corridor, stage above the flat seating area, folding chairs in neat rows to accommodate nearly three hundred persons. Around the edge fluted pillars gave additional otherworld aura, but the audience concentrated on the stage where, at the lectern,

163

Dick spoke. From some angles he was barely seen, short stature working against him, but the nubbin-like face was full of expression, his voice measured, fingers tracing Braille dots across pages he had prepared.

He could not discern his audience but even as he read the poem which began his "harp" the audience could have found even more meaning in the setting that evening. What were those words of reference? "I heard a blind girl, musing, say: 'I cannot see the stars, but I enfold within my soul a sky!' "

At the stage edge, up the front wall, across the front above where he stood, the wall was adorned with a series of plaster stars, part of the original design of the theater, eight up each side, thirteen across the top. A coincidence in itself of deeply poetic meaning.

"Life is the universe becoming aware of itself," he said. Even as you and I become cognizant of what has always been around us even though we may never before have realized it. Things appearing in our eye, in our mind. He read his poems, among them "We Three" which ended,

> *Serenely through this life I come*
> *That is my cosmos and my home,*
> *Giving such glory as I can . . .*
> *And hold my place: I am a man.*

The poem was of man, not merely of Dick Kinney, and yet every poem he read that chilly early winter evening had greatest meaning for his wife who listened across the town. He read poems of midnight, the sunrise, of love, of repentance, age, a poem for Walt Whitman, another of reading Zane Grey, of strength, snowfall—and of a robin with a crippled wing. When he was finished the entire audience joined in singing a "Happy Birthday" to the woman who was most in the poet's thought and who heard the merry tune from her bed.

"I wanted her to keep fighting. We both had been fighters all of our lives. We weren't going to stop now."

Evelyn determined to enroll at the Sorbonne, taking the trip alone, presenting herself before the admissions office, convincing them.

Evelyn and Dick leaving their wedding party to take a cab alone to the airport, to be on their own.

Dick minimizing arm touches of Rosemary as they walked to school.

Dick in Dr. Ketcham's office: "May I say something in my own behalf now?"

They would fight with all they had.

Through that winter they did, Dick now spending more and more time at the hospital where Evelyn had been taken for brief times in the summer and fall, now for a longer stay. Jeannie Ridenour driving him there, staying as well, going back each evening, somehow continuing with the demands of the school.

With Grecian references, Dick began at one time a poem to marigolds, a "salute" to them, calling the flower a "yellow phalanx" and the brief season of the flower, a "fight." He wrote:

> *Yellow phalanx, you guard my laughter;*
> *You stand up round it in a hollow circle:*
> *You chip off sadness with small swords from the*
> *tarnished surface of my heart.*
>
> *Here where the Persian winds assail you,*
> *And the Helot, frost, will soon betray you,*
> *You fight your small Thermopylae, and die.*

"You have to have a strong will." Dick knew that. "You don't just let things happen, you mold them for yourself."

It had been that way with Dick, fighting his own Thermopylae, and it was so with his wife.

You pray. Not, of course, as a public *thing,* not for the hundreds watching you like some novelty. "I'd call myself a reverent agnostic," says Dick. "I don't know all the answers, but I'm sure they exist." Dick was not much of a church-goer, and his answer was simple: He couldn't hear the sermon and for someone to manual a forty-five minute presentation was laborious beyond ordinary call. Even Ron Smith couldn't keep up with most ministers!

Many years later Dick told a friend the human being carries the built-in influences, the collated experiences of a billion years of life, that had the chain from amoeba to man been broken he would not have the inner resources, but that because it had not been broken there obviously were inner resources. "In moments of despair, when I sense this hidden reservoir behind the anguish and feel myself acknowledging not just affirming, 'I'm a helluva lot tougher than I think I am! Life itself is on my side.' I'm convinced the *sine qua non* resides within ourselves— built-in through a billion years. This knowledge does not spare us anguish or pain, which are a part of life. It does help us—or at least it has helped me—endure what anguish brings and look for resurging hope."

In 1811 William Cullen Bryant wrote of approaching death in his poem "Thanatopsis"; in all of its eighty-one lines he never mentions the word "God," and some felt this poem was atheistic—not so, God appears under many names. For Dick, the principle of creation is the sustaining force. Does it matter if he does not use the conventional phrasings?

Evelyn's faith was also a quiet one, her church one without a name. "Just Christians," her mother said. They called each other "friends" and sought a kind of "primitive Christianity" among themselves. She believed in her God, did not doubt God's omniscience.

Marcia Berman spent much time driving Dick to the hospital, staying with Evelyn when she was there or back on Elm Street. Mrs. Davis came regularly as did Mrs. Kinney. As the days wore on without much improvement, Evelyn did not discuss her future directly, but she knew what all the others knew. Lois understood the implications in her sister's statements: "She had her ways of telling us what she wanted done after she left us." Evelyn said, "Mother will never leave this house because she must raise my son."

Of Dorothy she said, "She will make a good nurse. See that she gets busy."

To Lois she admonished, "You've been through more schools and more courses with me than people with a master's degree. You go on and get your degree."

Evelyn once said to her husband, as he talked of circumstances of the future, "I can say there's no hope, but you must not agree with me. I can say it, not you." In other words, she wanted Dick to hold out, even if he said the condition was desperate he had to indicate hope as well.

From every adverse circumstance there can be inspiration; such realization helps give courage. In completing the Grecian account of the marigolds, Dick alluded to this as the poet plucks the flower—even in the mountaintop of its beautiful life—and then finds a time of reverence in its remembrance:

> *Am I a traitor also that I vanquish*
> *With predatory fingers from its stem*
> *One golden helmet?*

Black Boughs and Marigolds

I shall press it in a book with crimson bindings,
I shall place this book upon my study shelf,
And mark it "Hellas" with a silver pencil.

So when the white time comes to my own green
*   garden*
And the snow-beast snarls about my spirit-eaves,
And my heart grows numb with frost, I shall
*   remember.*

I shall remember on some white-haired morning,
By glint of fluttering firelight I shall answer
And draw Greek courage from one small gay ghost.

It's better to keep fighting, finding strength—even courage. When the flower is gone, the white-haired morning finally comes.

Christmas then, and days hastening on. Medical prognosis was allowing her only weeks now. To her mother, Dick wrote with a facing up to possibilities: "I realize we must face up to the possibilities of losing Evelyn. If we should, then I will need someone to help me bring Clark up. If you should want to be the someone and if you think your health would be strong enough, that would be lovely and fulfill Evelyn's hopes." There was no question of his sending Clark elsewhere: "I need Clark, and Clark needs a father."

Evelyn was brought back to 896 Elm; she wanted to be there. Dorothy was there now; with the family taking turns, Dick struggled to continue his work at the School, emotionally drained, however, for conversation with Evelyn diminished as her fingers weakened. He would hold her hand at bedside, speaking without response from her. The romantic monologues of just two years before now repeated, not by telephone, but with faces close, hands entwined, Evelyn listening.

March 5, 1965. Jeannie stopped by around nine that morning for her usual drive with Dick to the office. Evelyn had not moved during the night; there was no conversation. The doctor had come earlier that morning, using the Tellatouch with Dick.

In the car he asked a favor of Jeannie. "Drive around the block before going to the school." They drove, Jeannie stretching the block into three, then four, then circling again. She saw the tears coursing down his cheeks, felt them as her own.

A March day, overcast, windy—he felt the wind on his bare head, a touch that helped understanding—without a trace of springtime release. If we can get through the winters of our lives there are bright promises around corners. If we can get to them.

Jeannie's husband stopped by at the school. Dick asked, "Gene, why does God mete out so much to one man?" After long silence, Dick answered himself: "The only possible good is that he might through this help another."

Day stretched into afternoon, and there was a call asking him to come home as soon as possible. And were there ever five blocks that were as long and tedious as those that March afternoon?

At his wife's side, Dick touched her; Jeannie saw an eyelid flicker, the only motion anyone had seen during the day. This blind girl who had seen deeply into the heart of meaning in life, opening her eyelids in that moment as if to symbolize the search within her. And Dick, whose eyes had a veil drawn over them now for thirty-five years, reaching out for this touch, his fingers against hers.

Those at the bedside are confident that Evelyn recognized his touch. Mrs. Davis says that Evelyn tried to manual to him, even though she had not moved all day. He felt the faint finger movement in his hand.

169

The doctor turned, put his own fingers to the Tellatouch, placed Dick's other hand there, put the forefinger at the receiver, and slowly tapped out the message that death had now come to Evelyn in this little bungalow. She was thirty-two.

Dick's fingers flew now around her hand. He protested, "I feel her pulse!"

The Tellatouch again. "What you feel is your own."

In St. Louis when Dick first met this girl who sought more knowledge of literature he had put his hand to her waist to help guide him. "I guess I knew my attraction for her right from the start." He added, with typical flavor, "You might say it was a case of love at first touch!" Appropriately lighthearted for that grand moment—and prophetic for this last one.

Now, this final touch, and the hope that the pulse beating through his own veins might be hers instead.

In fifty-six more days they would have celebrated their third wedding anniversary.

At the memorial service in Winnetka the prayer said, in part, "We thank Thee for the Life Thou hast given, for her courage and her tenderness, for the words of truth and encouragement she spoke, for the deeds in love and service that she rendered, for her dreams and her aspirations, for ideals and convictions . . ."

Discouraged, feeling hopelessness a few days before her passing, Dick in the quiet of his office had put down words that gave testament to that grief—adding the hope he found. This poem was never offered for publication; it was written for just himself at that time. Some months later Don Hathaway came across it, misplaced among many other papers which had gone across Dick's desk, then to other offices. Reading the poem, Hathaway did not see Keats this time; no one but Dick Kinney and his own wrestlings:

AS BLACK BOUGHS

To grieve that you must go,
As dry leaves dread the snow;
To grieve when you have gone,
As black boughs mourn the sun . . .
Oh, rather, let my grief
Quicken the living leaf
Cherish the cherry bough
That blooms in your white brow!

Dick had her body taken to St. Louis for one day; burial would be in Chicago, but it was appropriate that she be identified as well with the city where she was born and raised. And so by train they went so that others might share their expressions of love.

Father Curtain remembered. And the entire convent out of which had come so many teachers for the diocese system. Evelyn was not Catholic, but they had given her the opportunity to teach; remembering, they closed the convent so that all might come to see her once again.

The nuns came by twos, introducing themselves to Mrs. Davis and then to Dick as names were manualed, the touch of their hands on him, then kneeling as they remembered her example, her teaching, her students, her gentle love first for a blind man in St. Louis and then for this rare deaf and blind man who had come to help her.

In Chicago the day was dark, chilly. Some seventy-five friends were in the cordon to the cemetery. Marcia Berman, who that day remembers Dick as a contemporary Job, a man who had suffered everything there is to suffer, volunteered to stay at home with Clark.

Dick was the only man there without a hat; a topcoat to fend off blustery winds, but head bare to feel the elements, the activity of nature even as they buried Evelyn who would never touch him again.

Unless it be through the wind itself.

At 896 Elm a portrait of Evelyn hangs above the fireplace; when you enter it dominates the room, an oil that captures much of her character. "Did you see the portrait of Evelyn?" Dick asks that of most newcomers who visit.

"Oh, yes. It's beautiful."

"I have it there so that Clark will always know what his mother looked like."

Ten years before her passing, while still a college student, she sensed the thought of deprivation and inadequacy which could come so easily to all handicapped persons. She wrote a poem in Braille, read it to a classmate who then jotted it down. The Braille sheet is long since gone, but the classmate, hearing of her death, remembered the poem and sent her copy to Mrs. Davis. Evelyn had written:

YOUR LIFE

You are in charge of a lifetime
Don't throw a moment away!
Happiness stems from progressions,
Sadness from idle decay.

Young hearts are aging too quickly
Too many warm loves grow cold.
Often we miss a bright rainbow
Seeking the rich pot of gold.

Dream for a better tomorrow
Strive for a better today.
You're in charge of a lifetime;
Live it in full while you may.

She, too, had not missed the "bright rainbow." Neither she nor her husband who wrote of rainbows in his poems.

A copy of the poem rests on the mantel, just below the portrait. They both remind Clark of how beautiful his mother was.

HORIZONS

He had his son. Nearly twenty-two months old now, to be raised by Evelyn's mother. She moved to the Elm Street home as deep recesses of Dick's thought would forever hold the view of Evelyn as before. What was missing was the touch of her hand, her fingers, someday to be replaced by those of his son.

Although the little house would never again be the happy place it had been during the early months of their married life there, Dick determined he would stay there, Clark would be raised in Winnetka. There was not a second's thought that there would be separation. Evelyn, too, had expressed the wish that Clark and his father remain together.

"As long as I have the strength God gives me I will stay." Mrs. Davis assumed her role with great love and admiration for her son-in-law and a realization of the challenges she faced. From Ohio, Dick's parents would come as often as possible, assist in every way. There was a great sense of understanding among all.

In the years since those first bleak days of late winter, 1965, the doors have opened wide for Dick Kinney to spur research into ways of assisting the deaf-blind throughout the world; overseas trips, which began with that historic talk to the World Council in Rome in 1959, continued the next year, have continued to pyramid since that time. At the time of Evelyn's passing there were fewer than 100 Tellatouch machines available anywhere; opportunities were nil for conversation between a deaf-blind and the "ordinary" person on the street. Very, very few persons today have ever seen a deaf-blind person, and fewer yet have ever learned a means of communicating efficiently with the deaf-blind. How many live their lives in hidden corners of families, shunted aside from normal emotion?

Ahead of Dick lay years of opportunity not only in promoting helpful educational discernments through the Hadley program, but also in giving his name and talent to the various other institutions concerned, especially the American Foundation for the Blind. The work to be done was staggering; by 1969, for instance, the Federal Bureau of Education for the Handicapped estimated that there were about 1,600 deaf-blind children in the United States —but that of that number fewer than one hundred had been "appropriately placed" for education and training.

They would all become adults someday with even greater needs for rehabilitation.

Working significantly first in regional efforts, then in a more national scope, the Anne Sullivan Macy Service in the 1960s was a significant project of the Industrial Home for the Blind. It worked for rehabilitation, mobilization of local efforts, development of good attitudes towards the deaf-blind, and research. Seeds were being sown in many ways. In 1967 the United States Congress called for the creation of a National Center for Deaf-Blind Youths and Adults, which officially began operation on June 28, 1969.

With the National Center, the Dick Kinneys of the

future would have a better chance with more research data to build on, better trained personnel, better attitudes. He followed all of their activities with great approval, perhaps thinking at the time of the close father-son relationship with Clark, "normal" with deaf-blind, wondering how it might be if their roles were interchanged. Fortunately, many others, the number growing daily, were confronting these possibilities as well.

"Romp with him," the AFB admonishes parents of a deaf-blind child; "treat him in play as much like others as possible. Let loose with him." Clark Kinney grew up in an environment which never discouraged his father from tussling with him. He opened picture books, having animals identified to him by others, memorizing page locations, showing animals to his son. If the two of them were on the floor reading, someone else was usually there to manual Clark's words as they spoke to each other. They laughed together, even cried when Clark placed fingers on his dad's cheek.

Three-dimensional clay figures were effective in Dick's teaching Clark. Recalling scenes from childhood, Dick would mold clay into forms that began, at least, to resemble animals—a cat, a dog, a horse. As he formed them, Clark would run fingers over them; Dick, sensing where Clark's fingers were, would tell him what part of the animal it was—leg, neck, tail, etc.

The next step they devised was to have Clark learn to put ears, legs, heads on the clay torsos which Dick fashioned. It was a triumph when Clark could say "ear" and touch his dad's ear as he said it; Dick, in return, fingered the clay ear and confirmed its right placement. Many evenings in those years were spent in this kind of activity, sometimes physically taxing for Dick, whose arthritic condition would recur. He did not let up, however, on the playtimes. And so an "ear" was a marvelous occasion.

They learned other games, mostly at Dick's contrivance. He named one of them "Animal March," an exciting game as Clark would come close to his father, who was on hands and knees on the floor. On cue from his grandmother, Clark would hop—brushing lightly on his father's shoulder as he did so.

"What animal?"

Dick never heard his son's questions, but the game was to guess the animal by its motions. The hopping movement was easy.

"Bunny!"

Clark laughed. "My daddy got it right!"

Next time the little boy was on his hands and knees, moving more slowly now, smoothly, but moving his rear in a definite motion.

Let's see, now. Dick's hands out, touching. Clark coming by again, giggling now and keeping his posterior in motion and hands felt the action.

Ah! Wagging of a tail. "Dog!" His voice was tremulous, excited, joyful, and Clark laughed again.

"Once somebody put a pillow on Clark's back as he walked by. I had to finger it quite a bit, a pillow, mind you, but I got the answer eventually—a camel with one hump!" A very innovative animal.

Well, that was a good one, but "Animal March" had a few more tricks to try out. One evening a visitor to the home, enjoying the game, took the same pillow, strapped it around Clark, had it on his *tummy* as he crept by. Quite a puzzle! But Dick's hands, touching, got the message. He smiled, said there were some smart people around the house.

"Mrs. Cow!"

It was a time of learning for both of them, of nature and

of touch. Earlier Clark had learned to identify animals from stuffed toys. On his father's lap he would pass them along, have his dad finger them, then point out characteristics. A time of growing up.

Mrs. Cow and the rest of the animal kingdom became parts of stories that Dick would tell. Years before, when finding out about magazines for the blind, Dick submitted many stories—mostly humorous—to such publications as *Skylark* and *Good Cheer,* both of them entirely in Braille. Now he had added incentive, writing for his own son; his stories were never submitted for publication, these were intended only to continue the bond between himself and Clark. His son was the most important audience he had. Drawing back on his store of recollections from his sighted days, he had material to fashion many stories. For example, the grand saga of Hoppy the Rabbit who was employed by a famous magician—and who became even more famous than his employer.

As Dick told it to Clark, time after time, it went like this:

"Hoppy was a fine little rabbit hired by the magician on television. He was the rabbit to be pulled out of a giant hat on the stage in front of a big audience.

"When the act was just beginning this one night, however, Hoppy the Rabbit fell asleep inside the lining of the giant hat; that is where he was supposed to hide until the magic wand was waved, and he knew it was time to pop out of the hat in his master's hand.

"Well, this night, fast asleep, he didn't know what the magician was doing. On the stage the magician was waving his magic wand and saying strange words and everybody was waiting breathlessly for the big trick, but nothing happened. Nothing at all! The rabbit didn't come out.

"The magician stooped over the giant hat to see what

the matter was, for the rabbit was to appear. He didn't see him, though, because of the lining. So, he leaned over a bit more to look in the giant hat, and then leaned over some more, and then some more, and then do you know what happened?

The magician fell right into the giant hat!

"Well! The noise wakened Hoppy the Rabbit who looked around inside the giant hat and saw the magician right there, standing on his head, the wind knocked out of him. Hoppy was a bit scared at that, as you can imagine, and he jumped right out of the hat! Right on television, mind you—and then Hoppy picked up the magic wand.

"He waved the magic wand several times, just like the magician had done, and by now the magician had gotten off his head and recovered. He scratched his head and then began to climb out of the hat, and pretty soon the whole television audience saw his head and then his shoulders and then all of him pop out of the hat."

Then Dick would conclude with something like this: "So you see, Clark, Hoppy became the very first rabbit in history to pull a *magician* out of a hat—and right on television!"

He never saw his son's eyes light up as the story progressed, never saw the smile, but Clark would squirm in his lap, then jostle him more, and Dick knew he was laughing.

Scenes of Dick and Clark at play were included in the movie "The Legacy of Anne Sullivan" which was produced in 1965, Helen Keller's devoted teacher-guide being remembered in the movie even as in the hearts of those who knew of her pioneering work.

Dick wrote his own tribute to Anne Sullivan Macy speaking in a poem the point of view of the deaf-blind children who, because of her patient, ceaseless teaching of Miss Keller, have benefited in both skills and attitudes. He wrote:

> *No song their mothers sang when they were young,*
> *No oriole fluting from the leaf-hung bough,*
> *Nor any syllable of any tongue,*
> *Nor natural song of speech, can reach them now.*
> *No light of long-remembered summer moon,*
> *Nor sunset, with its banners, marching west,*
> *Nor radiance of rainbow, glint of noon,*
> *Can pierce that dusk whereof they are possessed.*
> *Yet these laughing children and their blood*
> *Throbs with the lilt of springtime, leaps to know*
> *The swift, ecstatic moment: life is good!*
> *They walk with hope to greet it as they grow.*
> *Because you lived, Wise Teacher, love shines here,*
> *And minds, attuned to knowledge, learn to hear.*

Once again he had used the rainbow for a reference.

Dick made arrangements to go to South America, a journey he could not undertake during Evelyn's illness. His mission was to be an example, to convince men of government and finance that the deaf-blind in their countries could find self-sufficiency even as he had. The South American trip would be a significant undertaking.

Just weeks before it, however, another honor. His alma mater, long cognizant of his achievement, wanted to bestow an honorary degree on him that spring. A Doctor of Humane Letters degree. Could he arrange to come to campus, address the students, receive the degree?

He would be the second deaf-blind person in the nation so honored; Miss Keller had been so acclaimed by several other schools. Dick felt particularly proud that Mount Union College wanted to accord him the honor. Yes, he would be highly pleased to come. Joining him for the ceremony were his father and mother, Jeannie Ridenour— and Clark, now nearly three years old.

There were eleven hundred students enrolled then at Mount; about the same as when Dick had joined so many Korean war veterans fifteen years before. He would not attempt any campus strolls this time, however, for buildings had been added—three dormitories and a Science Hall. Bingham House was torn down.

The academic procession brought out full regalia; students who had never known of this Kinney fellow, some dignitary, watched with puzzled eyes as he came down the sloping aisle, head cocked a bit to one side, mouth moving with a brief smile showing, eyes appearing bright—a few knew they were artificial. This man about to get a degree beyond the lifetime reach of practically all in the audience: what made him so special?

For him it was homecoming, and perhaps the gentle slope of aisle reminded him in hesitant fragments of moments of the sloping corridor of an airport four hundred miles away where on a bright spring morning he held the arm of his bride and together reached a mountaintop.

Jeannie Ridenour accompanied Dick to the stage, manualed the words of praise. In listing some of his achievements, President Carl Bracy cited the Anne Sullivan Gold Medal for outstanding contribution to society, the Presidential citation, the Midland Authors awards. Bracy called him a "pioneer in the education of the doubly handicapped individuals, those who seek the fullest possible life through development of other senses and powers."

Dick stood by the lectern, Jeannie then giving him the message as the hood emblematic of the degree Doctor of Humane Letters was placed over him.

Then to his prepared remarks on the topic of "Together Against Blindness: of the Eyes, of the Mind." He spoke of the traditional "sixth sense" people have, particularly those who are blind. "New modern technology is actually giving us such a sense—a Technosense." He went on to predict new freedoms for the blind through technology. "Aided by electronic scanners, the blind will be reading inkprint as fluently as they now read Braille," he said. The cane would eventually become outmoded as the blind are guided by a "pen-sized sonar device capable of counting the sticks in a picket fence." For the deaf-blind a ring-sized device without external wires or batteries would eventually be able to convert the sounds around the deaf-blind into vibrations "so meaningful that even basic speech patterns should be simple to interpret."

Far-fetched? Just about as much so as the Tellatouch or the Tactile phone was twelve years before as he stood in the pay phone booth at the Sigma Alpha Epsilon house waiting for his nickel to come back as a warning that no one had been listening at the other end of the line.

He spoke of the little staff of seven people at the Hadley School when he became a staff member twelve years before, compared this to the new building, a staff of nearly fifty persons, and the three thousand students taught. He spoke of segregation in society: that fifty years before, nearly all blind children were educated, if at all, in specially segregated residence schools; that in 1966 more than half were attending public schools. And he spoke of "Technosense" as merely another means of getting *behind* the senses to the mind, the "reservoir and builder of all that is truly human in our lives."

Then he spoke of a dream that was about to come true. "A week from tomorrow, thanks to the generous confidence of the Hadley School and the 575 Lions Clubs of Illinois, who have named me Illinois Lions Envoy to the World, Jeannie Ridenour, my gifted secretary, and I will take off from Chicago's O'Hare Field on an around-the-world lecture tour that will enable me to meet for the first time face to face students whom I have taught by correspondence for years." Rotterdam, London, Athens, Tel Aviv, New Delhi, Tokyo were among the cities on his list.

To the Mount Union students, who warmed to this uneven voice speaking in terms of technology and humanity so skillfully, there was quickened interest and a ready response as he concluded by calling for termination of the worst blindness of all, that of spiritual blindness—"that has for generations prevented our seeing that we are all children of one God living on one planet and sharing one ultimate destiny."

As he ended, with emotion rising in the audience, he returned to a theme and a phrasing that has been a part of his rationale since childhood. He spoke of his personal faith that blindness of *any* kind—of the eyes, of the mind, of the spirit, can be overcome; he said, "Together, we *will* walk through the rain and through the rainbows."

Students, applauding, did not know the poem from which this line was derived.

At luncheon, after the morning convocation, they gave Clark a little sweatshirt with the Mount Union name lettered across the front and watched as he scrambled up to his daddy's lap and offered it to his hands so that the gift could be appreciated by his dad. And they watched as Clark moved about, squirming, letting his daddy know how pleased he was.

A telegram from former President Eisenhower spoke of his delight that Richard Kinney would now be Dr. Kinney; another from Vice President Hubert Humphrey spoke of the honor as a "milestone in the long upward stride of America's handicapped in achieving their highest individual potential." He said Kinney's award would encourage "countless citizens," both handicapped and normal.

Dick Kinney had much work to do: the astonishingly small number of Tellatouch machines in the world symbolized the dearth of global confrontation with deaf-blind communication.

A 25,000-mile tour in 1966 was a startling, goodwill, fact-finding jaunt during which he used the same title of his doctorate address in lectures. In the planning of the tour he held no concerns about his ability to be effective under stress of travel, of encounter with different cultures. He knew the motions of the flight, he had the ever-present assistance of extremely capable Jeannie Ridenour.

She was becoming one of the many miracles in his life; Cathy, Merry, Marcia, Julie—all were efficient, compassionate, understanding, skillful—but none was destined to play the global role that has been Jeannie's, nor to have the continuing years of close service. Her own family of three children in their formative, growing years, she nevertheless found the challenge of this travel too important to pass up. It was a chance to see the world, as some said, but more than that. How many have the chance to see and to hear the world not only for oneself but for another, too? Then, hers was a necessary temperament and tenacity; should she be needed, she could contact the Ghandis and the movie stars and the prospective donors—under Dick's bidding—without timidity. Further, her family, including husband Gene, whose career in education continued, never discouraged her from these ventures.

One is tempted to ponder, at least, the role that Evelyn would have played in the mushrooming series of goodwill trips. She had the tenacity, perseverance, personality to contribute much.

To Jeannie, however, fell the opportunity of manualist,

to see that the speaker journeyed safely; he could speak for himself beyond that.

A member of the Winnetka Lions Club for ten years, he was now being sent as goodwill ambassador to some sixty countries where there are Lions clubs. Their chief philanthropic project for many years had been in the area of sightsaving and rehabilitation of the blind. What more natural ambassador?

The trip included visits with Hadley branches in Europe, India, Jerusalem, South America. Before it concluded he had an audience with the Pope, a visit with Mrs. Ghandi, a bullfight in Spain, a chance to smell "dust, decay, death" in the Roman Colosseum, and to find that about all of the Tellatouch machines were confined to the United States. In Paris, a French war veteran, blinded in combat, used the machine to talk with Dick about discouragement. They talked about the Hadley School and the growing number of French signing up for correspondence courses in the English language.

"There is reason for the vast number and the interest in English," the veteran sighs. Slowly he types out the message: "It is because the blind in France have only one job opportunity—that of switchboard operator. If you can speak English you have an advantage over the other applicants."

A time to remember William Hadley. Broommaking? Good, steady employment there. Once, in a time he now wanted to forget, Dick had tried making potholders.

In Italy he discovers that one thousand blind men and women are telephone operators. He finds Jeannie manualing information from Dr. Matteo Alloco, Director of the Hadley branch in Florence, that the nation has a law there giving preference to qualified blind persons for these jobs. It is fine, as far as it goes. But is it far enough?

In Kenya there is difficulty with the government; Hadley courses are not recognized, there are certification problems. Dick promises to see that conditions are improved; he works with the Hadley office, the government, and the U.S. embassy. Three years later the Kenyan newspaper the *Daily Nation* reflects on his achievements, editorially referring to him as "the most remarkable man in America."

In Rotterdam Dick meets one of his own; Dr. Gerrit van der May, deaf-blind, was known to him through invention of the Tact-O-Phone. A blind mathematician who then lost his hearing in later life, van der May lived at home, received mathematical research problems over a special Braille phone message, later flashed answers to his laboratory fifty miles away.

In Spain Dick had the opportunity to meet two deaf-blind-mutes who know only Spanish. Now, that's quite an order for someone to unravel! Dick did not know Spanish, but the mutes, pressing out their own Spanish letters, having them translated by another, then picked up by Jeannie, and manualed to Dick, were able to communicate. The conversation required services of four other persons to transfer, interpret, translate!

Not all activities were so complex. At Madame Tussaud's Waxworks in London, Dick examines the figure of an English Bobby by touch—getting special permission. "Of course, the first thing I looked for was the famous police helmet that Bertie Wooster in the P. J. Wodehouse novels was always pinching." Then, walking on through the museum, Jeannie giving a cursory description, Dick pondered the simple ways the deaf-blind—and the blind —could have lives enriched. "If I can pat a statue it comes alive." How wonderful if every museum would put some specimens within reach so that the blind could study them tactically!

A copy of *Harp of Silence* is given Indian President, V. V. Giri; a useful, hour-long conference held with Krishna Menon, Cabinet Secretary of Law and Social Welfare. They were impressed. H. N. Mota, biographer of Ghandi, recognized the talents of Jeannie, speaks of her as "one of the amazing women of the world."

In New Delhi they have a productive visit with Indira Ghandi. She admitted blindness to be a major dilemma in India; greatly impressed with Dick's world knowledge, she found his perception intriguing. If he could be so advanced in thought and awareness, there was much yet to be accomplished with those similarly afflicted in India, even if their numbers were not fully known.

The *New Delhi Times,* covering a press conference, said, "Once in a while comes across a person whose dauntless courage, cheerfulness, and success in the face of physical disabilities inspire you to shout 'Bravo!' " It said that by Dick's presence in the country and his future labors it knew he was capable of, he would "bring good cheer and hope into the lives of the blind."

He met many; eight Kenyans taking courses from expanding Hadley overseas branches. He met others unexpectedly. For instance, one of the hostesses on a plane, aware of his handicaps, found extra thrill in coming up to him, touching his hand to signal that she wanted to give a message, then proceeded to manual—stiffly and slowly —words, forefinger out first with thumb touching the other three fingertips in his palm, then thumb and forefinger tip touching, the other fingertips in a straight line; finally the last three fingers bent sharply, forefinger outstretched, thumb at a natural "v" with forefinger—and repeated. "D-O-L-L."

"Well, what is this!" Dick pondered. "Feels like a real live doll to me!"

The hostess, basking in the victory, was delighted. She had played in "The Miracle Worker" in summer stock once, the story of Anne Sullivan. A few of the configurations came back to her "for real." She had never met a "real deaf-blind" before.

Perhaps one in 20,000 in the United States. A very rough estimate, close enough though to suggest that few persons have encountered the deaf-blind. In Asia the figure is one in 50,000, although the figure may stem from legal definitions more than actual numbers. The novelty of meeting the deaf-blind can lead to awkward moments. Perhaps it was emotion that led to such a circumstance in the visit with Pope Paul; he was so impressed with Dick that he clasped his hands, held on tightly as he spoke and, in so doing, made it utterly impossible for Jeannie to manual anything that was being said. Dick, in turn, had no indication of what he should be saying in response. Facing up to the problem, Jeannie finally unpried the hearty, genuine, all-hands grip and interceded with manualing. The Pope held as tightly to the other hand.

They flew to Tokyo, as Dick said, "in the wake of the Beatles and a typhoon," and found officials proud of rehabilitation services initiated for the blind; they were anxious to show this visiting dignitary their programs and results. The blind as masseurs were widely accepted in the nation, they told Dick; a special training program is given for the blind in this work, and would he like to have a firsthand experience with a talented blind masseur? "Sure, I'd like it very much," and so the next morning they took him with special guides—Jeannie did not go along for the treatment—where he underwent an invigorating session. Later, expressing appreciation, he said he'd take back the word of the high acceptance of the program. The Japanese were assuming real leadership here.

"And tell me, what *other* training programs do you have?"

There was an awkward pause.

"Well, what else do the blind do here?" he asked as Jeannie manualed no words at all. He did not need words to sense the situation, not unlike that which he had encountered in Italy, in Africa.

For him the trip had its light moments, fortunately, and its own peculiar challenges. For example, many years before, he had determined to learn something of swimming, had received instruction, understood the basics. It was in his childhood, of course, that the family cottage in Michigan brought the boat trips, fishing, water. He had not, however, learned to swim as a blind child. Laboriously he picked up rudiments while teaching at Hadley. When the trip neared its end, flying into Hawaii, Jeannie proposed that they go on to the beach; perhaps he might like the touch of the Pacific. He was enthusiastic, loved the feel of sand on his feet and, guided by Jeannie, was expectant about rushing into the waves. His description of what happened at Waikiki is better than any impartial observer could ever come up with:

I stretched forth my hand ingratiatingly as the first billow raced to meet me, but instead of shaking hands, it threw its arms around my shoulders, stood me on my elbow, and sent me crawling up the sands of Waikiki on my hands and knees —while successive billows played leap-frog over my shoulders . . . oh, well, let the kids go surf-boarding; we philosophers prefer to dream on the sunny beaches.

He was game. Back in Hong Kong he had written his mother that he had eaten birds' nest soup. "Very delicious.

It is based, I was told, on the swallow's saliva, which the bird uses instead of glue." Anticipating his mother's horrified reaction, he went on: "Before you turn pale, recall that honey is regurgitated by the bee."

In 1968 the World Council for the Welfare of the Blind convened in New Delhi, giving a signal honor to him. In that year, in June, the quiet, full life of Helen Keller, leader of all deaf-blind, came to a peaceful end. The woman whose name carried sponsorship which enabled Dick to return to his college education—and whose example had inspired so many others. The Council pondered the long list of dignitaries close to her and selected Dick to write the official eulogy to Helen Keller. Among other honors, Dick had been the recipient of the Helen Keller Gold Medal for Literary Excellence. He was asked now to write the eulogy and to read it at the opening session of this most noteworthy organization.

He almost did not make the trip. He wanted to go by boat this time, but found that officials of the *USS United States* were refusing him passage. "A deaf-blind person *cannot* be alone in one of our compartments. How could he ever get along?" They were adamant. And what about emergency procedures?

Senator Charles Percy of Illinois was contacted; could he do anything to convince them? Percy, who knew of Dick's achievements in many ways, was finally successful in convincing Cunard Lines, but only after much personal intervention.

Again with Jeannie along (but in the adjacent compartment) Dick journeyed to India for the eulogy:

I cannot think of the quiet passing of Helen Keller in her eighty-seventh year as other than the serene culmination of a truly happy life, magnificently lived. Writer, lecturer, philosopher, humanitarian, she demonstrated as has no other human being that to know is more important than to see; that to understand is more vital than to hear.

Once, as a very young man, I signed a Christmas greeting to Helen Keller, "One who owes you much." Miss Keller replied in a hand-written Braille note, "I cannot imagine what you owe me, but certainly my joy in this blessed day was sweetened by your message."

What do I owe her? Proof that the mind transcends the senses; example that teaches more eloquently than a thousand orations; practical help extended in innumerable ways through the programs she strengthened. Because Helen Keller was not satisfied by the foothills of knowledge, but pressed on to panoramic heights, I myself was heartened to continue my own education. The very scholarship that enabled me to complete my university studies was created in her honor. Through the whole fabric of her life and work runs a golden thread of inspiration from her words, her deeds. And yet I am but one of many who owe much—how very much!—to this woman who saw with her mind and heard with her heart. During the past half-century in America, every significant advance in the welfare of deaf-blind persons has been linked inextricably with her influence. Just this year, as if in commemoration of her passing, the United States government has assumed new responsibilities toward both the education of deaf-blind children and the training of deaf-blind adults.

He concluded his statement of tribute before the several hundred gathered that day in New Delhi by saying,

Helen Keller spoke for the blind who are deaf—yes, and for the blind who can hear. She spoke indeed for all human beings, everywhere, who aspire to their own full potential as contributing equals in the world's great community. Did a word need saying? She said it. Did a deed need doing? She did it. The causes she championed live on in her words. May her deeds live on in our own!

His continued emphasis on the role of the mind, the need for all persons to participate in the normal activities, were here coupled with the challenge to the rest of the world that that example be perpetuated in deed. Such stirring thoughts are easy enough to compile, but their impact will, by their very message, be felt only in the degree those who speak them provide example for them. That is why this man from the eastern hills of Ohio, from a village there, found himself in New Delhi sharing them. He had known deprivation, humiliation, inadequacy, yet had made in his own way his deeds as well as his words ring out for others to know.

Annette Dinsmore prophetically had said when he was graduated from Mount Union College, "You have the golden touch of the power of words and through this gift you can influence people so that they will realize that deaf-blindness does not in itself mean an insurmountable barrier."

To a young woman who sought counsel regarding some poetry she had written, poetry of despair, he had written, "I wouldn't presume to advise you on how to handle anguish or on the philosophy of despair. True, I am not unacquainted with both emotions. But every person's response to them must come from within—actually does come from within."

What do "normal" people have to learn from a Dick Kinney as we search for the answers within ourselves? In a way, it may come down to the word "discovery" with our minds. Discovery happens with the senses as well, the lesson from him is that of touch. Touching can be crude, violent on occasion; at best it is a discovery of what already has been all around us.

Consider Dick Kinney flying in a Boeing 747 jetliner around the globe today, perhaps in his capacity as consultant for the Department of Health, Education, and Welfare, or the State Department's Bureau of Cultural Affairs; trips taken in the continuing cause of welfare for the handicapped. Sensing the motion of the airliner, sensing movement through still or turbulent skies, he knows that what is taking place is only that which can take place out of a set of conditions already established. Nothing of our basic physical laws has ever changed in the world around us; we simply have been learning, discovering more about them. Mankind could have flown centuries before the Christian era; every law of physics, thermodynamics, aerodynamics, every law of gravity, propulsion, action, and reaction was then the same as it is today.

We just hadn't discovered the laws.

Dick speaks of this in its most philosophical sense: "Life is the universe striving toward consciousness of its own being. Evolution is life moving toward a more perfect consciousness. Every individual, conscious life is a little window through which the universe contemplates itself."

There are so many, diverse ways in which human understanding is evidenced in this man's life. Named Associate Director of the ever growing Hadley school in 1969—the year he received the public service award of *Dialogue* magazine—he continued his missionary work. On May 13, 1969, he was on board the *USS United States* on the way to Paris for the International Council of Correspondence Education sessions, when Mamie Eisenhower, hearing that he was on the ship, invited him to visit with her.

"Youthful in face, fragile in body, gowned in a lovely black, cut-velvet dress," Dick described her, thanks to

Jeannie's helpful manualing. He and Mamie covered a range of topics by Tellatouch; yes, Mamie recalled the President's conversations with Dick a decade before. At times during the evening Mamie seemed tired, almost melancholy, and he longed to be of help.

In Paris he spoke of the Hadley School's widening spheres, used his own case as proof of success of home-study courses, met Maurice Chevalier and induced him to become a Hadley sponsor. Then on to Monaco for an audience with Princess Grace in the royal palace. She had invited many guests to meet this remarkable American; she translated into French his answers to their questions about the deaf-blind—and became another sponsor of the Hadley program. His role as public relations director had many facets!

Finally on that trip a visit to Coupvray and the Louis Braille museum; there he attended ceremonies for sixteen Hadley students being awarded certificates of completion of courses.

"You learn never to be downhearted around him." Liz West, a Hadley School volunteer worker says this. "He has incredible strength . . . and a humility that is not mousey." She has learned from his humorous and indomitable spirit. "One time he needed to get into the car near the curb. It is difficult for him to maneuver in certain positions; the combination of curb, door position, and the seat made it more than he could usually manage."

But Liz smiles as she continues: "It didn't bother him, even with the recurring arthritic condition in his legs. He invented a new device and said to me, 'Have you ever seen my backward cannonball?' "

"No, what's that?"

"It's either spectacular—or fatal! So far, it's been the former!"

With that he catapulted himself backwards into the car in a type of reverse leap during which he could have hit his head or even missed the seat. But he made it; with great aplomb he leaned out the window and asked, "Will you allow me to open the other door for you, my dear?"

Nobody gets depressed around *him*. Liz is firm in her conviction.

Attitudes. For him a sense of humor, not a depressing fatalism is necessary. George Shearing, agreeing with Dick in a discussion on this point, said, "If I lose my sense of humor, I'll probably live only another hour."

Lightheartedness can be highly relevant; as an administrator responsible for the financial stability of an institution solely dependent upon contributions for its continued existence, Dick has the right to be light and relevant when, in a speech, he said:

From the physical standpoint, mobility was at one time regarded as a more or less unrelated grouping of specialties useful in overcoming blindness. Champions of the guided dog raised dogs. Champions of the long cane raised cane. Some blind people scorned both dog and cane and placed their faith in echo perception. Many blind gentlemen of my acquaintance still think you can't beat the right arm of a pretty girl. Come to think of it, I am sure that the first nonprofit institution to advertise "Go-Go Girls for the Blind" will have solved all its fund-raising problems!

As yet, Hadley School has not ventured into this possibility.

Dick's activities cover a wide range—from traveling to New York to visit IBM, interviewing and urging the company to underwrite a computer programming course in 1970, to writing a memo of caution regarding zoning regulations near the Hadley building. He works in diverse involvements daily. Perhaps it's a concern for a new reference librarian, one who will scour inkprint texts for all those suitable for Braille—then, again, he may be writing a memo about a questionable judgment of one of the English staff in evaluating student papers.

With budgets he is in his prime, they become pawns in a new type of chess match. He delights in knowing that the school ends one year twenty-eight dollars to the good. Later he speaks of his support-hunting trip to Sweden as one in which he will "speak softly and carry a big check."

He likes word choices. Writing of clouds to a colleague, he finished by saying, "I hope you haven't taken me too cirriously!"

His sense of humor has practical applications. In Ireland on a search for governmental assistance for the blind recently, he and Jeannie decided to visit the Blarney Stone. However, to reach it required a hike of about eight hundred steps—narrow, circular steps winding upwards without any landing along the way. His legs wouldn't permit it, and yet he was so close. What to do?

"Well, we decided to resort to great strategy. I had Jeannie take a good picture of the tower—and then I kissed the camera. That way we fulfilled the tradition without effort!"

He can laugh readily. Meg Kuhn, another of his secretaries, and Dick were eating in a Houston restaurant one noon when a man from a nearby table observed the manualing and came over to inquire what it meant. Finding the story, he was overwhelmed with the "celebrity." He began to pump Dick's hands, tell him—in ordinary voice and therefore totally unknown to Dick—the story of his family, his children, his job. He rambled. "Quite excited, really," Meg says. She took Dick's other hand, began to manual—not what the visitor was saying, however, but some uncomplimentary observations about his manner, his ego, his personality. Dick chuckled throughout the long oration but the visitor continued to pump Dick's hand throughout the life story.

Little human-interest dramas unfold about him continually. At the Willow Club in Winnetka waitresses know him, vie for taking care of him. I thought I might be able to pick up some more anecdotes and asked the waitress who was getting the order from Jeannie but busily fussing about Dick. Had she waited on him before?

"Oh, all year. We all love this man."

I asked about the first time she waited on him; was there any problem?

"I'll never forget it. I had worked here for several months and had the hardest time making a parfait—waitresses make their own. I'd get it looking like anything but a real parfait. Well, this one time I was successful! It was a beautiful job, just the way a parfait should look. I was really *proud* when I brought it in the room and set it there in front of him . . . and then realized that he couldn't even *see* it. And I couldn't *tell* him how beautiful it was! Of all people it had to be *him*. I nearly cried."

Jeannie hastened to manual this to him.

"I don't know about the parfait," he told the waitress, "but *you* look beautiful!"

He has said that he doesn't believe in laughing *at* anyone, including himself, for such laughter is simply cruelty in disguise. "But to laugh *with* others at life's frolicsome foibles or hilarious incongruities—ah, that's art! That's psychotherapy!"

Recently, while playing a game of Scrabble with him, I found how his "incongruities" could so easily creep into the conversation. He uses a specially constructed board, with indentations instead of marked squares, so that blocks can be dropped into them as he forms words, builds on others. In addition, the letter blocks are identified in Braille dots as well as inkprint. After each move on my part his hands would fan out across the board, relocating again each piece and thus discovering what additions had been made. After a particularly flashy burst of wordage on my part, his hands again darted out, a tap on his wrist signalling that I was done. He ultimately discovered the long word I had created with its high point value.

"Aha!" he exclaimed. "You were really busy when I wasn't looking!"

Such lightheartedness is psychotherapy for those around him as well.

Humor is a good object lesson in using our full mental capacities; most humor is based on ambiguity, the double-meaning statement. We laugh at something because in the *wrong* context it makes sense. Much of writing creatively is putting ideas in context seriously, to compare, to write metaphorically. You learn of these things when you are around Dick Kinney. To survive without two key senses demands that his intellect, his thinking process, be creative. Liz West tells of a simple incident:

"One day Dick and I were chatting during the noon hour; he mentioned the kind of day it was and added, 'I heard geese honking overhead this morning.' "

It was his way of saying, of course, that spring was coming—in his mind's eye.

Because of his ability to *relate* circumstances—one thing in terms of another—he goes beyond the void world as we might think of the deaf-blind. Recently a group decided to give him a surprise party. More than fifteen people were gathered in the room after the dinner hour, there to celebrate some occasion which Dick was unaware of. After waiting about fifteen minutes in the room, they hushed (why? habit, I suppose) as they were told he was coming down the hallway, accompanied by Keith Kartman, an audiologist. Then the two of them entered the room and without hesitation Dick stopped short.

"Ha! It's a surprise party!"

Now, *how* could he tell? Kartman and others in the room, although delighted, were a bit chagrined at the fact that their surprise was discovered so readily. How did he know?

He had sensed one thing, put it in terms of another. In context.

In this case, the first was smoke. The amount of it in the air. Dick then estimated the number to be "a dozen or so."

In piecing together the raw elements of the perpetual detective game unfolding in his life, there are differences of opinion as to how much of it is game-playing, how much the same as the rest of us would experience. Kartman cites a time in the competition of a chess match when Dick and others were playing chess wizard Bobby Fischer. Dick lasted forty-four moves and was ahead at that time, but made one sloppy move then which ended the game. Observing the match, Kartman concluded that Dick needs as much of this kind of "release" activity as possible, but that it is never a tense, "do-or-die" affair. Still, he wonders: "I cannot believe that Kinney is as happy as his outward facade would lead us to think."

Perhaps it goes back to the sense of humor.

Suppose you had never heard a sound for twenty years, that regular checking proved only a continuing void. Then, one day, a faint—very faint—glimmer of something. Was it a sound? Would you clutch at it? Scream out in release of emotion? Or would you cry in bitter fleeting of that moment?

Kartman tests Dick yearly for some vestige, however faint, of hearing. In the specially designed room sounds are electronically produced. In the middle of that barren laboratory room several years ago, seated on a lone chair, sat Dr. Richard Kinney, as he had in other years. Told to remain still, listen intently. Then, outside the heavily walled room dials are twisted, volume increases of one lone sound. Through the single window the audiologist watches intently for any reaction. Nothing. More dials now, volume increasing. 100 decibels, 250 cycles, a terrifying noise that could shatter the minds of "normal" people; highest sound attainable with the complex electronic equipment—and then the figure on the chair twitches! Cocks his head slightly! Sound suddenly turned off, Kartman rushes in.

"I think maybe I heard something!—Right at the end!" The highest, most terrifying noise possible.

"It sounded like the key of C."

Kartman shook his head in wonder, then told Dick that at the very end the frightening sound, beyond the mode any ordinary ear could ever stand, was, indeed, in the key of C.

At which Dick bounced up and grinned. "How about that? I've got perfect pitch!"

And for weeks he proudly shared that conclusion with friends.

In the years that have gone by since his marriage and the loss of Evelyn, he has been part of a widening influence of the Hadley School, capped by a fiftieth anniversary of the institution in 1970. Dick assumed most of the daily operations of the school by that time, making salary judgments, smoothing wrinkles of emotions when problems arise, deciding public relations campaigns, evaluating staff, and lecturing. Today he holds the position of Executive Director of the School.

What of deaf-blind education? Since 1954, when he received his college diploma, there have been a handful of others who have earned the college degree while deaf-blind. Doors are opening; they have been since the Amercan Foundation for the Blind report in 1954 spoke of the "inherent right of every deaf-blind child to have an education."

Today the National Center for Deaf-Blind Youths is an extension of the Industrial Home for the Blind in Brooklyn. Since creation of the Center by Congress in 1967 it has been operated by the IHB. Philosophically, it rests on the right to freedom from needless dependence, the right to personal identity, the right for opportunity to contribute to a person's community, the right to respect for the dignity of the individual and the worth of his contribution.

The Center, which serves by direct enrollment on the grounds, not by correspondence, is today doing much innovative teaching, some from Dick Kinney's example. Lou Bettica, director, says, "Proud as we are of the great strides of the National Center, I realize that the great feat of Richard Kinney is that he did it, for the most part, on his own."

Dick's role by example is encouraged for others. To the Committee on Services for the Deaf-Blind of the World Council he recommended that films on deaf-blindness be circulated as widely as possible throughout the world, especially by TV, but "still better are live TV appearances by deaf-blind persons capable of discussing topics other than deaf-blindness—that is, capable of presenting a 'fully rounded citizen' image."

To show the deaf-blind as normal, functioning persons, rather than oddities—that is the best promotion of all.

It is what his life has been.

In the Colombian capital of Bogota Dick brought his presence into the life of an eleven-year-old deaf-blind girl who was attending a church school. As he received a report on the school's services to the blind, the little girl sat close to him, clasping his hand, giving evidence mostly of pantomime nature, but Dick was pleased. "The essential point was that the school evidences a progressive spirit and is sincerely interested in carrying forward this first formal training of a deaf-blind child in Colombia."

Such education was also a possibility in Paraguay and certainly in Argentina where the Helen Keller Institute for the Blind is located at Cordoba; two deaf-blind children are being educated there.

The American Foundation for the Blind has continually stepped up its own programs. Films and booklets to help teach the deaf-blind and to help others understand their problems have been available through the Foundation since 1951. The Foundation and the Perkins School for the Blind in Massachusetts helped develop college courses for those who wished to become teachers of the blind and the deaf-blind.

Research into rehabilitation of the deaf-blind is going on at the National Center, Bob Smithdas involved in many activities there as Dick Kinney is halfway across the continent. Each sees his role as symbolic and practical leaders of the philanthropy for the deaf-blind. It is Kinney, however, who has been the driving force on the World Council, who has traveled the globe, not only prodding governments, seeking the deaf-blind, but most of all through such trips *showing* the dominion the deaf-blind can have.

The role of the Hadley School must be stressed; it is

not a competitor of the American Foundation, the Industrial Home, the National Center. Each serves a different function. Of them, only Hadley functions by correspondence, in the home of the blind or deaf-blind. The Foundation supports a wide range of research and services but offers no courses. Hadley does. The Center teaches deaf-blind youths mobility of many kinds, but this is done at the Center. As a young boy Dick went to a school to learn Braille; today it can be learned at home.

Having gone through the agony of losing sight and hearing over a period of years, Dick knew firsthand the psychological and practical problems facing those in middle years who lose key senses and must make profound adjustments to life-style. His book *Independent Living Without Sight and Hearing,* which came as a result of the course with the same title that evolved in the mid-1960s, was first available only to the deaf-blind themselves—in Braille. Today it is in inkprint, too, and of tremendous value to the families of those who become deaf-blind.

Making adjustments is something Dick knows; his work today emphasizes this. His trips overseas require Jeannie or Meg or other secretaries for purposes of conversation with authorities and for full awareness of the variety of papers, addresses, and commentaries made during meetings. He has, however, full confidence in his ability to get around without them on some flights and other transportation; he was doing so with taxi cabs back at Mount Union twenty years ago. It is foolish for him to try to walk down a city street when he is devoid of perception of traffic patterns, but once in a taxi or plane he is capable, thank you, of taking care of himself. His first "solo" flight was in 1958 and others have followed, a recent one from Hanover, Germany. He had been there on a Council on the Welfare for the Blind special session for Deaf-Blind. His associate was Jeannie, who stayed over for a few days. Stewardesses, who were German, were completely informed of his situation, all airline personnel briefed by Jeannie before she left the cabin after getting him seated. There were no problems anticipated on the German airline.

Well, no *problems,* just "opportunities," as he had said at Mount Union's commencement! We'll see how flexible a man he is! After some hours aloft, he found himself being tapped on the wrist, hand directing him to the receiving end of the Tellatouch always at his side.

"Oh? Stewardess?" His finger in place now.

And the word "c-o-p-p-e-r" is being spelled out.

He must have gotten the message incorrectly. His face shows puzzlement. Again the German stewardess spelled out the word, setting in motion the Sherlock Holmes opportunity—take the clues and solve the riddle. Well, let's see. In flight now for about three hours—Braille watch confirms that—plus a German stewardess who knows some English but might have trouble with spelling, trying to say *something* with "copper." She can *speak* English; spelling may be the problem. Maybe she has a dictionary somewhere, trying to be helpful. Trying to figure out a key word—the Tellatouch awes many people—with correct spelling. Individual letters were punched out slowly, deliberately. C-o-p-p-e-r. What is copper, what's made of it? tubing? Plumbing?—Why, *that's* what she's after! Plumbing!

"Ya, ya, fraulein! Show me the way!"

She was taking good care of him.

On another flight, Air France this time, a stewardess, having been briefed thoroughly about his condition, showed her admiration. She bought him a drink, used the Tellatouch to say she was paying for it. "My pleasure!" she said.

So many reactions!

In Buenos Aires, a government spokesman said, "His qualities as a teacher, as a person who has overcome great personal difficulties, and simply as a friendly, intelligent human being charmed all who met him." In Asuncion, Paraguay, officials said, "No other foreign visitor has ever received such wide and abundant newspaper coverage."

To the outsider, there are some startling conclusions to be reached about deprivation. When you think about it, loss of sight and hearing creates its own type of vacuum— but opens up as well potentials never before realized. The reverse of deprivation offers marvelous opportunities for establishing priorities. Helen Keller once spoke of the things she would see if she could have her sight for just three days.

On the first day, a very busy one, she would call on all her dear friends and look into their faces. "Imprinting upon my mind the outward evidences of the beauty that is within them." She would also walk through a forest, "intoxicate" her eyes on nature. "That night," she wrote, "I think I should not be able to sleep."

On the second day she would glow with the dawn, then go to museums, first those on anthropology, then those on art. She would "try to probe into the soul of man through his art."

In the evening it would be the theater—Shakespeare, Pavlova, the beauty of rhythmic movement.

On the third day, "I would stand on a busy corner, merely looking at people, trying by sight of them to understand something of their daily lives." Then a stroll down Fifth Avenue, look at colors, then the slums, factories, parks. Then, as night came on that final day what would she choose? Some awesome excursion? She decided, "Perhaps there are many serious pursuits to which I should devote the few remaining hours, but I am afraid I should on that evening of the last day again run to the theater, to a hilariously funny play, so that I might appreciate the overtones of comedy in the human spirit."

Something to think about.

In South America, during Dick's journeys, they were turning back, unopened, Braille transcribers and Tella-touch machines; customs officials fearful they were some type of weaponry. In Chile the blind were unable to vote in any elections because, as a government authority noted, "They can't see the ballot."

And throughout the world some people go about daily unaware of the discoveries of the dawn and dusk, the stars above, and the sights and sounds around them.

There is a difference between being blind—and wearing blinders.

The vacuum of deaf-blindness takes away, at the same time, some things that were never really necessary. Consider the dynamics of much social and racial unrest these days. "We're the only ones," Dick says, *"fully* liberated from the thought of either racial superiority or inferiority. The deaf-blind are absolute equals."

He is right in another way, too.

The loss of sight and hearing affects all cultural backgrounds; studies are quite inadequate at this stage, but there is no evidence at hand that one cultural heritage, one national descent or even one gender is a factor in the frequency of affliction.

And when you're standing in a fourteenth-floor apartment on Chicago's south side, your eyes sweeping across row after row of identical apartment houses like sentries against the lake edge, then listen to the bright chatter of a woman seated in her cluttered, small study you begin to understand.

Geraldine Lawhorn is black. She is deaf. She is blind. An employee of the Hadley School, she is the only teacher in the world of a correspondence course on "Independent Living Without Sight and Hearing." Fifty-seven deaf-blind persons have taken the course thus far, each averaging about ten months for completion.

The course, Dick's brainchild, is aimed primarily at adults who are losing sight and hearing.

It uses his textbook, the only one of its kind.

On her desk, Jerrie Lawhorn moves fingertips across a Braille letter received recently. "This course was truly an exciting experience for me," it says. She smiles, hurries on to share the rest of the letter. "When I think that I'll lose my hearing I still have chills down my spine, but not as much as before. At least I know there is a way."

The writer is a man in his thirties. He has a wife and two small children. He is blind and has been told to make "adjustments" in his daily life because he will join the ranks of the deaf-blind soon.

Miss Lawhorn went through the same sequence in her lifetime as Dick had—first a loss of sight while still in grade school, then a loss of hearing while in her late teens. For her, a career of stage presentations—monologues, primarily—helped sustain personality. When their paths first crossed at the Industrial Home for the Blind in 1950 —where Dick was receiving a brief training for campus return—their friendship began by correspondence. Later she incorporated many of Dick's poems in her programs. She was fortunate to have a wise, loving mother who refused to see her daughter as second-class in any manner; if she were handicapped in one way, she would excel in another. Classroom recitations impressed others and from then on, through guidance in love and persistent effort, she found an independent career in the theater.

"When we were casting about for a teacher for the Independent Living course," says Dick, "I thought of Geraldine; her life is full of independent thinking and living."

The endorsement is not a conventional administrator-teacher one; the puzzle, the detective game is never ordinary for the deaf-blind. The mind is what counts. Geraldine emphasizes, "I'm working in my teaching to have students see—yes, that's the word!—that our *minds* can dominate, that materially we express only what our minds are doing. If we could improve ourselves mentally to our potentials, if we fully realized our mental might, there just wouldn't be any time left to think and fret about the body."

There are fine lines of distinction with regard to the working of the mind. Bravery and bravado: same words? Hardly; the first is genuine, the second a put-on. Yet they come so close in expression. Courage and stubbornness. Same? Hardly. Yet Geraldine uses these words in describing her colleague:

"He has the courage to continue and yet it is a kind of stubbornness. The deaf-blind *have* to be stubborn. If we aren't stubborn, people just don't believe us!"

Jerrie uses an adapted "pager" by touch for a doorbell. When the bell is pushed a shortwave radio beam activates a vibrating pager she always carries with her. It's somewhat experimental, first used by Dick who passed it on to her. Courage and stubbornness are hers, too. In fact, Dick claims there is more "human drama" with her than with himself.

He refers to the situation of Jerrie living with her elderly mother—the person who had done so much to make her daughter's life meaningful—now slowed considerably. The mother is unable to take care of herself. Should they try to live without others, just the two of them in the apartment?

At night Jerrie pins their blankets together as they sleep in beds side by side; if her mother needs any assistance during the night, she follows the edge of her blanket to Jerrie's and tugs slightly. Jerrie, knowing every inch of the tiny four-room apartment, responds readily to her mother's slightest touch—the manual is difficult for her mother to do now—and takes care of the household.

It all goes back to the mind. If the deaf-blind have learned to use their intellect to its potential, their step ahead of the "normal" may be interpreted by some as stubbornness, when, in fact, it is not an unthinking rigidity but a courageous, logical stubbornness exceeding normal bounds.

Miss Lawhorn finds that persistence is rooted in her own perspective about handicaps. "I have never lost my faith that I might be able to see and hear again, but the more I use my mind, the more I sense God's creation on a spiritual basis, the less concern I have for materiality."

You leave her apartment as she goes in deliberate steps to the kitchen to check on the evening meal, a chuck roast browning on the stove. At first you assume she is merely looking at it to see if it is done, but then, as you step into the hallway, you become aware of the paint from one room, the chicken frying in another, onions in the next, even someone's body odor in the cramped elevator, and you realize again that you have never fully appreciated the awesome ways your mind can function despite deprivations.

And you ask yourself, "How courageous—how stubborn—have I ever had to be?"

You think of lines written by Robert Smithdas on courage:

all things that toil against despair, yet gleam;
something of joy from life's deep, hidden springs.

"Hidden springs" unfortunately remain untapped by many individuals through fear, timidity, futility. Foes such as these are what the deaf-blind have to conquer. Courting a girl in a windowed studio because you have to. Don't be concerned about other people. Have your "romantic monologues" on the long-distance phone because you must. Do what must be done, act out your own personality.

Back in 1959, on board the *USS Independence* headed for Rome where he was to be the first deaf-blind person to address the World Council, Dick Kinney was in the dining room with his mother who manualed the fact that the ship's orchestra was involved in a quiz show, entertainment wherein passengers are to name tunes to challenge the band, see if they could play them. "Beat the Band" was the old radio show version with the Kay Kyser band, Dick remembered. The competition got to him, seated at a far table, eating, never hearing the music.

Could anyone stump the band? By golly, he would like to!

Mrs. Kinney was not enthusiastic about his participation. She manualed that others hadn't succeeded. "Can I call out a tune now?" was all he asked.

She tapped him.

"Give My Love To Nellie Jack!"

Everyone in the salon turned, then waited for the band to play it—but none in the band could recall the tune. The leader said, "You'll have to come up here and sing it for us—otherwise we'll know there was no such a song!"

Hope Kinney was embarrassed, hesitant. She manualed what was said, but discouraged him from getting up and going before the crowd. Not so for him! It was a good game—and he knew all the answers; so, with his mother guiding, he walked to the bandstand and in front of the diners began to sing—at his mother's cue—the old bar-room song, "Give my love to Nellie Jack . . . and kiss her once for me . . ."

I have heard Dick reenact this scene, complete with the singing; it is as bad as the Geisers thought of his early morning shower songs . . . but the awareness of his will-ingness—stubbornness—to do what he could do, to be himself regardless of adversity made it beautiful. I have stayed overnight at the little house at 896 Elm, wakened to the sounds of Dick Kinney singing in his bedroom across the hall. "The Star Spangled Banner" sung by a man who knows not how the melody is coming out is a bit of a rude encounter at 7 A.M. But I learned quickly that it was something to be grateful for. "If he starts sing-ing in the morning," explains Mrs. Davis, "it's a sign he's feeling all right. The tune may be pretty bad, but it's music to my ears."

It's a signal. Like whistling in the corridors of East Sparta High School, saying, "Here I come!"

In a time when his hearing was still a fact of life, such noisemaking could serve another purpose. Evelyn Kinney once wrote that "It is not true that the blind hear better. It is just that they train themselves to listen more carefully. A lot of people are amazed that a blind person does not run into a solid object, but they could do the same thing, without seeing, if they would train their ears to the sound of footsteps, to hear the bounce-back of objects."

Perhaps that is another reason why he whistled some-times when walking lonely corridors, inventing his own means of identifying the world about him. In an age of mechanization, in a time of greater invention and scientific exploitation, individuality seems less frequent; the cry is for greater assertion of oneself; we stress this, but seldom find it. Perhaps Dick has an answer for all of us in contemplation of the mechanization: "Inventions give us wider range of selectivity, therefore more individuals can define themselves."

Tact-O-Phone, Tellatouch, Braille scribers, electronic pagers were all items for making his own selectivity, giving him greater choice, just as bounce-back of sounds gives greater awareness. What is real individuality? Dick said, "The prerequisite for an individual is to grant the right for others to be individuals."

Going over his morning mail he may find correspondence from Shyana, a young deaf-blind girl of India—from a cultured, well-to-do family. She has written of her new Tellatouch. Dick wonders how many there are in India who live out their lives in corners of hovels, shunned by their deaf-blindness. He ponders. Shyana was lucky, her family could make contacts. There is much work to be done for the others.

Reports from Amelia Kelley of Pittsburgh—deaf-blind, she assists the Hadley staff by correspondence. She had once said "deaf-blind persons, if left to their own devices, will inevitably deteriorate mentally and physically." You've got to be doing something!

It reminds Dick of the young physician, age 34, going blind and dying. Conversing with Dick via Tellatouch, he spoke of pending suicide. Dick had other ideas. "Put your hearing to work," he insisted. The physician did, goaded by the conversation, conducting valuable research on children's heartbeats, studying birth defects, in the intervening months before his death.

Today the Hadley School for the Blind—promoted, administered, inspired in significant measure by its Executive Director—employs some fifty instructors, 90 percent of whom are blind. At any given time the school has about twenty-five hundred students on its rolls, but actually lists four thousand, for many who have enrolled stay on after completing courses to use tapes, records, or other services.

Branch operations, with teachers in residence, are located in France, Spain, Italy, Greece, Israel, Kenya, Latin America. Some three hundred are taking courses in Latin America, three hundred in Europe, one hundred in Asia, nearly one hundred in Africa, about thirteen hundred in North America. The new Department of Studies for the Deaf-Blind continues its search for helping the newly deaf-blind, beginning with a simple but highly important "spelling board"—a small board with raised letters. By touching letters with fingers of the person who is deaf-blind, words are spelled and silent communication begun. It's a beginning; Braille and the manual and a host of other aids will follow. For the person newly deaf-blind the simplest approach is psychologically necessary.

A course in "Using the Abacus" is highly popular, enabling the blind to solve arithmetical problems more rapidly and accurately than the average sighted person can with pencil and paper. A dozen are enrolled in the new computer programming course; 110 students are in the radio course (fourteen lessons on tape), and the Hadley Radio Society has its own station. In the vestibule of the handsome school building a new telephone switchboard, developed by Illinois Bell, uses a light-sensitive electronic probe that emits audible signals when moved over the board to tell the blind operator what line is being utilized.

Dick's "Independent Living" course sparkles with wit and insight suitable for all persons. His message is basic, obvious, yet so sorely needed to be stated. It is to be yourself, use the talents you have, adapt to circumstances, and go on from there. "Why did this happen to *me?*" is painfully asked by the deaf-blind, but he admonishes not to spend our time dwelling on possible answers. He prefers to quote the golfer who said, "I always play the ball from where it lies"—never wasting time fretting about past mistakes or ill fortune. "The golfer does not say, 'If only that tree were not blocking my path.' He accepts the fact that the tree is there and starts planning how to hit the ball over or around it."

It is done by finding the greater achievement possible with the mind. He puts it this way in the course:

A parakeet has keener sight than man. A dog has sharper hearing. A mink has a better sense of smell. Yet a man puts the parakeet in a cage, chains the dog in a kennel, and drapes the mink over his wife's shoulders. Why?

A rhinoceros is larger than a man, a tiger more fierce, a gorilla far stronger. Yet the rhinoceros, the tiger, and the gorilla are behind bars at the zoo, looking out. The man is on the outside, looking in. Why?

Because the man has a better mind. He can observe and draw inferences; remember and learn from experience—both from his own and from that of others; foresee the future; imagine solutions; invent tools; communicate ideas through language; accumulate knowledge through written records; cooperate with others to achieve goals he could not attain by himself.

His book, now in inkprint, is available for use by the families of the deaf-blind. For the legions of deaf or blind who lose a second sense midway through their careers, the book and course get into the home where they are usually needed desperately. Children and teens can be sent to the National Center, but many older folks withdraw to the security of their home; for them correspondence work is invaluable.

We are all children of discovery, putting together conclusions about absolutes in our lives from these ephemeral, relative experiences which accumulate to determine perspective and philosophy. Those whose lives have crossed paths with Dick Kinney have been enriched in many ways. We are all children at times. For Rosemary Kinney, in the early days when her brother was blind and the object of special trips, examinations, and attentions, the activity became an element of envy.

"Children don't recognize the factors involved," she says. "He went off on glamorous trips to distant hospitals while I stayed with what we termed 'hired girls.' We both placed great importance on our trophy collections, but nothing in mine could approach the spent bullet he brought back from his visit to the site of the battle of Gettysburg."

Reflecting more on the perspective of time, she continued, "It never occurred to me to wonder what went on within Johns Hopkins examinations rooms during that same trip."

Until touched by these experiences personally, few of us do ponder the additional elements of stress and anguish within our fellow beings. Our perspective is too limited.

Wagons and carts rattled by the peasant farm home of the Braille family in the early nineteenth century. On one occasion, Louis—just four or five years old—commented to his sister, Marie, "Francois is driving by. One of his oxen is lame."

Marie was surprised—for, upon looking, she became aware that the blind boy was correct. She asked, "How could you know?"

He answered with one word. "Listen."

A century and a half later people came and went in the assembly hall where a conference was being held. Dick Kinney, silent for some time, spoke out suddenly.

"Hope you got a good picture of me!"

The photographer was dumbfounded. "He's deaf and blind," he said to Dick's companion. "How could he know?"

She manualed the question.

He answered with one word. "Heat."

And we can all grow up and become more aware. For Dick and his son the years are full of awarenesses now between them—for the first time. Clark's vocabulary had to mature before manualed conversation could truly be two-way. Years of groping for full expression of thought through scattered jabs and hurried pokes become, now, thoughtfully manualed descriptions and comments. Games are becoming more meaningful as Clark widens his vocabulary, comes to grips with broader horizons of his thought. Today it is on the Chicago Cubs, his school, neighborhood. And home.

"May I have a drink?"

Clark goes to the kitchen, returns with one for his dad. "Thanks, Mom."

A hurried tap on the right wrist.

"Oh! It's Clark. Thank *you!*"

He is fortunate to have a loving father. Dick was, in turn, blessed to have loving parents who would sacrifice anything for his good. Illness forced his mother to assume a lesser role in some of the years, but she remained the same solid, resolute person that enabled Dick to avoid the limitations of self-pity as a young adult. Her strong, confident example is worthy of the "University of Courage." His father, who died in 1966, was not as much in the forefront of Dick's many activities, but his own quiet, determined philosophy was equally essential to acquiring confidence. Ron Smith felt that Hobart Kinney was the final source of much of Dick's decision-making in the formative years, although friends would not have realized this.

And what a confident person is Mrs. Davis! "The Lord gives me what I must do." She speaks almost in an off-hand manner, but there has been great endeavor on her part to provide a happy, harmonious atmosphere when Dick is returned home after each working day.

We have come through this story with emphasis on awareness. For the deaf-blind in the future there is promising research into refinements of the sonic aids; some experimental equipment can now translate spoken words into highly efficient vibrations, some incorporating Braille patterns, others the "Visotomer" geometry approach to letter configuration. From the past comes a seemingly simple tactile approach—devised by Sophia Alcorn for the American Foundation for the Blind: using two persons born deaf and blind, she developed a vibration method of reading speech by having the deaf-blind place his hand on the cheek of the speaker and interpret vowels, consonants, eventually words by the movements of facial muscles. One of the persons involved, Winthrop "Tad" Chapman, helps promote this technique through the Hadley School today, a technique called "Tadoma" in recognition of his work.

One of the newer aids for the blind is particularly helpful as they walk. Working on the principle of a bat's perception, it uses a microphone-like device which emits a steady tone when no object is near in its line. An earplug is worn as it is held. For the deaf-blind, conversion to a vibrating response would serve as readily.

Today "mobility instructors" are being trained to teach the wide range of alternatives—and there exists the potential of transplants for the deaf to bring the world of sound again to their apprehension. People like Dick Kinney will stress unceasingly the need for awareness of *all* the possibilities, not for anyone to sit resignedly in his rocking chair waiting for some ignoble end. Dick's role is that of a catalyst, to get things going in the lives of other deaf-blind and blind persons. He puts it this way: "Sometimes we can crystallize the determination to try. Often we can help them try more wisely, more successfully. We can blow on the coals without claiming either to have lighted the fire or grown the wood."

The determination to try. In 1950 he outlined his approach to self-sufficiency in a letter.

On the evening of November 8 I shall speak before the Gideons of Canton, Ohio. The theme of my talk will be that problems are opportunities, with the history of Braille as the prime example.

After the meeting members of my audience will be given the opportunity to buy copies of my poetry brochure "Flight of Arrows" which sells for fifty cents a copy. This technique is used effectively by many professional lecturers. After this talk I shall also distribute souvenir cards bearing the letters of the Braille alphabet. On the back of each card will appear the words "Richard Kinney's Magazine Service, phone East Sparta 8683."

Thus each of my vocational objectives will be spear-headed a little nearer victory—self-support—in the course of one evening.

I believe that a deaf-blind person can make his own way as a useful and contributing member of society. With your help I hope to prove it.

The letter was to Richard Wood of the Ohio State Rehabilitation Service for the Blind. He attended the Gideon meeting that night. Out of it came, eventually, college, channels, continuing awareness of his potential. Started by himself. The grief of earlier years molded into achievement.

During those wonderful college days he had written of the rainbow:

> *I am the band that binds the locks*
> *Of stormclouds when the rain,*
> *Unloosened by loud thundershocks,*
> *Has swept its silver stain*
> *Over rocks and rills and woodland hills,*
> *Till the high blue bowl of the heaven thrills*
> *Above the broad-hinged plain.*
>
> *I hallow the grief that goes before,*
> *I leaven with love the hate;*
> *When rough winds havoc and loud clouds war*
> *And fierce rains fall, I wait.*
> *For when stormclouds part, I etch my art*
> *Like a quenchless hope in the heaven's heart—*
> *Or a smile on the lips of Fate!*

Fate itself had to smile for him. And because it did for him, it did for so many others.

He likes to look to stars and sky in expressing himself. Helping a young person who had asked guidance, he wrote:

I myself choose what might be called philosophical double vision. By that I mean that I reserve absolute freedom to speculate on and make judgments about ultimate reality, the nature of the universe, the meaning of life. My attitude is that of an absorbed, expectant observer eager to learn more, always ready to revise, steadily refining hypotheses, reaching out for further conclusions.

The other half of the double vision is the practical one of how to live my life and what daily goals to seek. It does not need to explain all—just guide me and lend coherence to my life. My favorite precept is "mutual life enhancement." To enhance one's own life in such a way that the enhancement also adds to the happiness and welfare of others—that's the goal involving emotional satisfaction and a challenging use of intelligence.

It was Don Hathaway who said, "Dick Kinney sees more deeply than any of us, he hears more than any of us."

I am sure of this. Still, his efforts to stay above utter depression must be supreme. Amelia Kelley has said that one of the worst features of deaf-blindness is the isolation it imposes on its victims. "This is not purely a physical thing. It is an isolation of the spirit as well, which nothing can reach or dispell." Then, almost with a nod in Dick's direction, she says, "Those who are imaginative and gregarious by nature feel this aloneness more keenly than do their more stolid fellows."

But Dick will not dwell on the morbid. Other aspects of his life are his topics as he shares his thoughts and recollections. A patch of buttercups in a field across the street in East Sparta . . . and a rainbow. "Yes, I can remember the rainbow over a shed across the railroad track."

He has seen both the rain and the rainbow, and has held firmly to the bright symbol of a clearer day. From another lover of the open countryside comes assurance of the divinity of the rainbow's implications. English poet Ralph Hodgson, who said so many kind things of Dick's poems and had written in his journal, following their chat, that "some things have to be believed to be seen," also said in one of his poems

God loves an idle rainbow
no less than labouring seas.

221

The quietness and beauty of a rainbow, the energetic thrust of the sea—both expressions of a freedom that mankind seeks. He had gone through the water and found the sun splashing through it in many colors. Many friends have helped, hands to be reached out to, hands reaching out to him. And the slim, firm hands of a girl who loved him enough in their brief years together to sustain an endless bond. His solitary achievement in finding at-oneness with his own sense of the divine has in a measure found the rainbow in his son, his poetry, his work.

How does one conclude this account of such a remarkable man?

Perhaps an incident at the Mexico City airport recently captures much of his persevering spirit. He had attended sessions there in behalf of the deaf-blind. Meg Kuhn of the Hadley staff was his secretary-guide. Ready to return, he found customs procedures snarling her efforts to accompany him to the actual boarding of the airplane. Security had been tightened, and officials would not permit her to leave the terminal, to accompany him on the walk towards the ramp to the plane and into the seating. She was to stay over—Dick had flown alone many times—but she was desperately trying to convey explanations of Dick's condition to the plane's personnel. Once seated and explanations given, he could go to Chicago where he was to be met. But, no, the agent would not allow her beyond the gate; no, he would take no message on board; no, they could not bring a hostess into the terminal; no, he would not assist this strange passenger.

Frantically Meg manualed the situation to Dick as passers-by watched in curiosity. Dick smiled, assured her things would work out.

She tried again to go along, past the gate, to the plane,

but the men were adamant. Rules and new security. Then the crowd moving past, time gone. She manualed her failure. What could they do? Should she try to hail another passenger?

Man must do what he is to do. The dictum was clear. It had gotten him this far. "I'll make it, Meg. I'll make it. Get me started."

After she turned him slightly and manualed the approximate distance to the ramp, he began his solitary walk. The gate closed. Ahead, the trek to the plane's stairway and boarding. He could not speak Spanish, none on board knew of his total adversity, but he kept on walking slowly, alone, analyzing sparse clues, touches. It was not the terrazzo floor of O'Hare and there was no bride at his side to lean on. On past the terminal gates and the people—was his thought back to that wonderful day of the taxi ride from the Sheraton, of the gentle climb leading to the exhilarating touch and song of the Golden Gate Bridge —and of the bathroom heroics?

He was, now, almost shuffling with burden of weak knees touching in slow cadence. He once had told Meg, "I have only one handicap—the arthritis."

Keeping a cane ahead of him, holding on to the ever present Tellatouch in his other hand, he went towards the plane, towards his home and his son, and his precious work.

In his darkest days, nearly thirty years before, when deprived of his second sense he asked in one of his poems:

> *. . . shall the poet carol*
> *of sunshine in the rain,*
> *of rainbows over peril*
> *of Spring that comes again?*

223

In his own remarkable way Richard Kinney was already answering, even as he confidently struggled to board the plane.

He was answering by making his own rainbow for the others who would come to see it, if only within their hearts.